FRUGAL LIVING

A Guide On How To Save Money And Live More
With A frugal Lifestyle

(Improve Quality of Life Through Simple, Frugal
Living)

Mark Howard

Published by Oliver Leish

Mark Howard

Frugal Living: A Guide On How To Save Money And Live More With A frugal Lifestyle (Improve Quality of Life Through Simple, Frugal Living)

ISBN 978-1-77485-152-4

Legal & Disclaimer

The information contained in this book is not designed to replace or take the place of any form of medicine or professional medical advice. The information in this book has been provided for educational and entertainment purposes only.

The information contained in this book has been compiled from sources deemed reliable, and it is accurate to the best of the Author's knowledge; however, the Author cannot guarantee its accuracy and validity and cannot be held liable for any errors or omissions. Changes are periodically made to this book. You must consult your doctor or get professional medical advice before using any of the suggested remedies, techniques, or information in this book.

Upon using the information contained in this book, you agree to hold harmless the Author from and against any damages, costs, and expenses, including any legal fees potentially resulting from the application of any of the information provided by this guide. This disclaimer applies to any damages or injury caused by the use and application, whether directly or indirectly, of any advice or information presented, whether for breach of contract, tort, negligence, personal injury, criminal intent, or under any other cause of action.

You agree to accept all risks of using the information presented inside this book. You need to consult a professional medical practitioner in order to ensure you are both able and healthy enough to participate in this program.

Table of Contents

Introduction

You can make a financial change if you are struggling to make ends meets and finding yourself in more debt to pay for your daily needs. Although it may seem daunting, if you have the right strategies and stick to a financial plan, it will be surprisingly easy.

This book will provide you with a comprehensive guide for a complete financial overhaul, from debt relief to retirement planning and everything else in between. This book will also teach you how to conduct a professional financial assessment to determine what your options are and create a plan that suits your needs. You won't have to spend any extra money on a professional financial adviser after reading this guide to frugal lifestyle.

These seven chapters will guide you through the entire process, from your initial financial evaluation to the creation of your final budget. This will help you not only get debt-free but also financially secure. The following chapters will teach you:

* How to conduct a comprehensive assessment of your financial situation and see the first signs of the greatest drains on income

* Strategies to get out of debt permanently

* Planning for retirement with a low income

* How to create an investment portfolio that works for you.

* How to build a savings account to feel secure in difficult times

You can make simple lifestyle changes to reduce clutter, save money and feel happier in your life.

* How to put everything you've learned together into a realistic budget that will help get your finances on track

Keep reading to discover how you can change your life today.

Chapter 1: The Not-So-Fabulous Life Of Luxury

The disadvantages of living in richness

A relaxing vacation with the whole family that will last for a whole week in an exotic island which is out of the country. The latest model of the most expensive brand of cellular phone in the market. A very big mansion with 20 rooms, a swimming pool, a golf course and its own helicopter pad. A walk-in closet full of designer clothes, shoes, bags and accessories that cost a whole lifetime worth of your paycheck. State of the art appliances and technology for your home. International schools with mind blowing tuition fees for the kids. A garage full of luxurious and very expensive vintage cars and race cars. A hotel suite that will make you feel like a princess and a royalty. A plane ticket that entitles you to the best accommodation. These are just some of the things that people from the upper class enjoy in life and get as privileges. Sounds like a fabulous dream, right?

A lot of people aspire to have and live a kind life that the rich gets to experience. Gorgeous clothes, expensive cars, lavish banquets, hosting the kind of parties that get featured in magazines and newspapers,huge and massive homes– everyone wants all of these materials things. Everyone wants a kind of life in which everything is easy, everything that you have is of the best quality and everything that you see is yours or can be yours in just one single transaction.

But even if this kind of life may seem posh to us and even if it may seem very appealing and truly enticing, it is not just all glamour and glitter and nice. There are also a lot of issues that being rich can incur. Like normal people, the rich also deals with a lot of problems, sometimes even bigger ones that the ordinary people or the commoners encounter.

A lot of people would instantly trade places with the elite if given the chance.

However, what some people don't realize is that being rich can be problematic too. How? Read on and find out what the advantages of being rich are and you might want to reconsider wanting this kind of life.

1.   Luxury living can result to debt.

It is a false belief that rich people do not have any debt. Although being rich can translate into having a lot of money and properties, it can also translate into having a lot of liabilities. This may sound unbelievable but this is actually a reality. The reason why living too much in luxury is not good is because some rich people and members of the elite community tend to overspend on things that are only considered as wants and compromise their savings just so they can have anything and everything that they desire. They hold extravagant parties and wear extremely expensive clothes. Not to generalize, but there are also some who want to acquire much material things until they do not realize that they no longer have any money left. Some people become too comfortable with the fact that they have money and that they have a lot of it to the point that they no longer keep track of their expenses. There are a lot of lottery winners who experienced this dilemma.

So in the end, these people, who are used to the luxurious life, wind up having debts. Mind you, not only rich people have this tendency; so can members from the lower class. All of us can be quite compulsive when it comes to buying and acquiring things especially if we know that we have a lot of money to spend. So it really takes a great deal of discipline in order to become smart with your finances.

There is nothing wrong with spending a lot as long as you are still on track with your assets and your spending. There is nothing wrong with splurging from time to time. But as we all know, spending beyond what you are capable of spending is not good and will never be good. It can only get you into trouble and can put your properties in great jeopardy.

2.   You will have a lot of things to guard.

This reason why being rich can sometimes be problematic is pretty funny but it is actually pretty logical. If you have a lot of things and you have a lot of assets or property, you will not just be popular to the people around you but you will be an attractive target to robbers and thieves. You will become the Holy Grail for burglars and criminals and they will seek you until they get what they want from you.

As said previously, a lot of people want to live luxuriously and almost everyone desires the fabulous life. However, only a few people, who are fortunate enough, get to experience it and live that way. That is why, it certainly cannot be avoided that there are people who have bad intentions towards the elites. Being rich does not only mean living the easy life. It can also mean having to guard all of your properties so that they will not be taken away from you. Due to this reason, sometimes,it is better to have just enough because at least, you can rest easy and have a good night's sleep compared to when you have much to spare but in return, you always have to feel scared that someone would come into the dead of the night and rob you.

True enough, having a lot of property can make you shine like the most expensive diamond in the whole wide world and make you feel absolutely grand. However, you can never be too dauntless especially that there are people everywhere who get attracted to the radiance that diamonds emit and would stop at nothing just to get it, even if it means having to rob it from someone else.

3.   Having a lot of things can incur great expenses.

It has been a common adage that the only constant thing in this world is change. Everything changes– the environment and the surroundings, the people around us, plans for the future, our aspirations in life, and even the things that claim to last for a lifetime. Everything undergoes the process of change and nothing can escape this. It may sound poetic and may only be suitable for romance stories but in dealing with property and assets, both monetary and materially, we have to put this fact in mind.

If you are rich and have a lot of possessions, these possessions will eventually depreciate through time. Your appliances will undergo breakage. Your clothes will need to be sewn and repaired if suddenly damaged due to chemical reactions each time they are dry-cleaned and pressed after every use. Your shoes will eventually wear out. It will come a time when your expensive watches will stop working. Your cars will require monthly maintenance to ensure its great performance on the road. Your homes had to be renovated or fixed for repairs and improvements. The bottom line is, having a lot of things that undergo changes can also mean having a great deal of expenses. You have to pay for the maintenance and for the repair, if necessary, of your things. Not only that. You will also have to spend a lot of money for electricity if ever you have a really big home with lots and lots of appliances. And if electricity bills are not enough already, you will still have to pay for phone bills for all of your cellular phones, and gasoline for your cars to name a few.

Being rich really means having a lot. Not only having a lot of money and property, but also having a lot of bills to pay.

4.   Having a lot does not always equate to being happy.

There are a lot of Hollywood actors and actresses who can be considered as eligible to have a spot in the list of the wealthiest people in the whole world. There are a lot of businessmen whose wealth is so unimaginable that they can practically buy a country. There are millionaires and billionaires who have assets that are equivalent to the wealth of an entire nation. But, a lot of them are not really happy with the way they live their lives. A lot of actors and actresses commit suicide due to depression even if there are a lot of people who idolize them and even if theyhave a lot of expensive things. There are billionaires who have a lot of money but do not have the love that only a complete family can give. There are businessmen who are so popular to other people but are nobodies to their own children. There are wealthy people who can afford any food and drink that they like but couldn't have them because their illness forbids them to enjoy these simple pleasures. There are politicians who have a lot of houses in different places but don't truly experience what it is like to have a home.

This is the saddest part of being rich. Sometimes, you gain fame and property but lose your family, your loved ones and the more important things in the process. The simple things in life that make ordinary people happy get replaced with material things that breaks and perishes through time. True, you have a lot of things, a big house, anda lot of cars to use but what is the purpose of these things if you don't have anyone to share your things with, a wife, or a husband, or children to make the big house feel a little less empty, or even the strength to even drive your cars out of the garage? Sometimes, material things just cannot compensate for severed ties and relationships. It cannot replace a loved one that you lost. It certainly cannot fill the emptiness and the gap that only true love can patch up. It certainly cannot stop a deteriorating health.

All of us dream of becoming rich and to live a luxurious life. But, we sometimes forget to consider the fact that being rich can have problems too. We sometimes don't see the sadness of being rich; but having no one special to share it with because we often get blinded by the glitz and glamour of luxury makes everything worthless.

Chapter 2: Why Choose A Minimalist Lifestyle?

Would you like to make your home feel like a restful haven? Slowly over time you may have collected so many treasures that the charm they once had has lost its appeal. Perhaps you want to invite company over for dinner yet your home is in disorder, or the productivity at your home business has suffered due to misplaced papers. By tossing out trash, donating items, and putting the rest in their proper place, you'll discover you have more time to do the things that matter most.

The true cost of clutter:

You continually struggle to find your car keys, tools, and basic clothing staples. This costs you time and money while pursuing these lost items.

If your home is messy, you may feel embarrassed when someone arrives at your door.

If you have a home business, clutter affects your productivity. When your workspace is overcrowded, it's more challenging to stay focused on the task at hand.

Guests and family members can feel the visual noise when there is domestic disarray; the clutter becomes a distraction.

Extreme cases include compulsive hording. Failing to keep trash, newspapers, magazines, or spoiled food out of the house creates an unsanitary living space. In case of an emergency, exit pathways might be obstructed.

So what do you need to do? Remove all unnecessary visual noise

Starting in the room of your choice, set a timer for 15-30 minutes; make a quick decision about each item. You now have 3 action choices to take for every piece of clutter.

1) Toss trash into a designated bag.

2) Place giveaway items into a box.

3) Misplaced items which belong in another room go into a laundry basket for easier carrying.

1. Trash / recycling

Grab two trash bags. Sort out between recycling and garbage. Immediately toss after making a decision.

2. Giveaway

Put items to be donated into a box marked "giveaway." Often the Salvation Army or other local charity organization will pick up the items directly from your front porch.

If there isn't an organization that will do so free of charge, place larger items such as furniture at the curb with a "free" sign attached.

Most likely these items will be gladly claimed by a passerby. Sites such as Freecyle.org give you a platform to announce your giveaway items. Never allow guilt to keep you hanging onto possessions you don't absolutely need or love.

3. Return misplaced items

Once the room has been cleaned up, all that should remain is the laundry basket. Grab your basket filled with items to be placed in another room and immediately put them away.

The best way to eliminate clutter is to prevent it from entering in the first place

When you have fewer possessions there is no longer a need to organize as often. Keep wish lists handy for yourself and family members so when a birthday or holiday arrives you're prepared to share your gift choices.

This way you'll be more likely to receive gifts that don't become clutter, or are genuinely useful. One way to encourage people to ask you for a wish list is to ask them for theirs! Set an approximate dollar amount you both feel comfortable with. Some minimalists even go so far as to forgo the gift exchange entirely.

Be careful when accepting giveaway objects. Diligently guard against garage sales and inheritance items without a compelling purpose.

So now that you have gone through the clutter it is time to adopt a minimalist lifestyle, which is the simplest way to combat clutter. There are dozens of excellent blogs written on the subjects of simplicity and minimalist living. Make it a daily routine to read one post and get motivated.

Let's start with some general tips.

If you find it overwhelming to set aside large chunks of time for decluttering, set your timer for 15-30 minutes - or try a 25 minute Pomodoro timer. Then do one room a day until you have finished the house.

The moment you know a shirt no longer fits, toss it into a giveaway box. Keep this box accessible!

Buy fewer, yet higher quality items.

Don't be too rigid. If you see an item that belongs in another location, deal with it right then. Don't fuss over placing it in a laundry basket with other items to be relocated.

Once you have a room looking nice, take a natural daylight photograph to serve as your inspiration for maintenance. Enjoy a sense of satisfaction knowing you will be more productive, and you can proudly welcome guests into your restful home..

Chapter 3: First Person: I'm Learning To Live With Less

As a business professional, I've had the good fortune of making a decent living for many years. I'm thankful for my job and the money that it brings me. However, over the years I fell into the habit of spending whatever I made. If my income went up, so did my spending. Today, I'm thinking about things in a whole different light. I'm learning to live with less and loving it.

• Housing

I bought my first home at the ripe old age of 19. In those days, it was all about "trading up." I was taught that you got a starter home and bought the ugliest house in the best neighborhood. Then you went about making improvements so you could sell it and save money until you could get your bigger and better dream home.

The problem was that I kept trading up. I never seemed to find my dream home. I've moved so many times in the past 30 years, it would make your head spin just thinking about it. Yes, I fell into the trap of thinking "bigger is better" and I sized my homes accordingly. Today, however, I'm looking to downsize. I'm thinking about 850 square feet or less would do me just fine. Why would I really need more? I can only use so much and it's just more to clean, insure and pay taxes on. I'm ready for a change.

• Cars

I've gone through my years of wanting a bigger, faster or flashy car. I'm a little bit of a car nut, so I've owned just about everything from a restored Corvette to a big old SUV. Today, I drive a Kia Soul and delight in its 30 miles-to-the-gallon gas consumption. I've learned that my car is just a vehicle that gets me from Point A to

B. It doesn't have to attract attention. When we get a little older, we get a little wiser – or so it seems.

• Clothing and Jewelry

My spending habits have drastically changed over the years. Although I'm happy to say that my clothing and jewelry budget were the first to go quite some time ago. When I was in my teens and twenties, it was all about what outfit to wear and what jewelry I wanted to buy next. After amassing a generous collection, I finally asked myself, "What more do you really need?" That put a halt to a lot of needless spending.

• Toys

I still get a hankering for toys now and then. As an artist and DIY fanatic, I'm constantly tempted to go out and buy the newest tools of the trade. But, these days I'm playing a different tune. I'm leaning more on recycling and upcycling for my projects and keeping more money in my pocket.

Learning to live with less has been a hard transition for me. But, I'm working at it. Maybe by the time I'm 60, I won't eat out as often, either. We'll see.

Chapter 4: Budgeting

If your eyes glaze over every time you hear the word 'budget,' you probably don't have a handle on your money. Budgets get a bad rap because they aren't the boring, drudge-filled documents that most people think they are. They're magical, beautiful things that put you back in control of your finances, but only if you stick to them.

There are lots of different budgeting methods you can use, but some are more effective than others. A budget is just a plan for your money, every penny of it. By telling your money where it needs to go every month, you can make sure that you stay in control of your finances.

Budgeting isn't difficult, but it may take you a few months to get used to making a budget that works for your needs. You need to know how much you earn, so you'll know what you can afford to allocate for everything you put on your budget. What goes on a budget? Anything you plan on spending money on, including your impulse purchases.

Look at what money you'll need to spend during your next pay period. Don't wait until payday to do this; look at what you received on your last paycheck and use that as a guide. If you know you'll bring home, say $500, for example, and you know you have a $300 car payment due plus you need to buy groceries, you'll need to budget for both of those. You can't spend more than $200 on groceries, because of the car payment, so pick an amount that is practical.

Obviously, this is just an example, because real life never breaks down that smoothly. More than likely, you'll have some weeks where you have more bills than income, and others where you have more money than bills. The goal is to spread out that 'excess' money to cover those weeks where you really need it. Ideally, you'll also have a category for unexpected expenses.

If you have money left over in your budget, assign it a job. Savings is the most practical choice because it's good to have a safety net should an emergency pop up. But you also need to plan ahead for larger, predictable expenses, like auto insurance, taxes, and even Christmas shopping.

You can't fall into the trap of thinking that just because you have money left over in your checking account after you have paid your bills, you can spend that money willy-nilly. You need to realize that you need to plan ahead for those larger expenses and unexpected expenses, too. If you'd like to be able just to spend whenever you want on whatever you want, create a budget item for it. Set yourself a budget of $X.XX every pay period just for impulse spending, and spend it without feeling guilty, as long as you've budgeted all your necessities, too.

The beauty of budgeting is that it eliminates any nasty surprises if you do it right. If your car breaks down unexpectedly, but you have been planning ahead and putting away money every pay period for car repairs, you don't have to panic and put it on a credit card, digging your debt hole even deeper.

If you're wondering how you can keep track of every dollar you spend, you are in luck, because thanks to this wondrous age of technology that we live in, there are several great apps and pieces of software that make budgeting painless and even a little fun.

YNAB (You Need a Budget)

YNAB is a very popular piece of paid software that makes budgeting super simple. It stands for 'you need a budget,' and its principles are simple. First, you have to give every dollar you have a 'job.' Then, you have to make sure that you are including those long-term, larger expenses in your budgeting plans. (Sound familiar so far? It's the basis of any reliable budget!).

Once you know where your money needs to go, you can learn to make small adjustments, giving yourself permission to mess up now and then, but in a controlled way. At the end of the day, budgeting is just controlled chaos, because every single person budgets for different things, and you may not budget the same way from month to month or even week to week. It's okay to make changes to your budget by moving money from one budget category to another; it's not okay to overspend every month and fall back on your credit cards.

The Envelope System

Another tried, and true method of budgeting is the envelope system. Lots of people use this system--in fact, your parents probably did, too. Financial guru Dave Ramsey promotes it, and it's easy to see why. It's just easy, period.

The envelope system of budgeting simply involves taking all or most of your cash out of every paycheck and distributing among envelopes that have been earmarked for different things in your budget. For example, you might have an envelope for groceries, one for car expenses, one for utilities, one for eating out, etc. Whatever you plan on spending your money on, give it an envelope. Then, you only spend what is in that envelope, and nothing more. Once the money runs out of one envelope, you can decide whether you want to pull money from another envelope (adjust your budget) or not.

Some apps let you do this virtually, so rather than having actual envelopes, you set up budget categories in the app and 'fund' the budget by telling the app how much you have to spend. You track every purchase and expense in the app so that you can stay within your budget at all times.

Since most people have smartphones, these apps and software programs make it super easy to keep track of your budget anywhere you go, so you don't have any excuse to overspend other than a lack of self-control or emergency, but even emergencies can be dealt with through budgeting for them. (See how awesome budgets are now?)

A few envelope budgeting style apps to try are Betterhaves, Goodbudget Budget Planner, and the MoneyWell app. However, of these three, only Betterhaves is free.

If you want a budgeting app that links to your checking, savings and credit card accounts, you can try the YNAB, which has a software fee, or Mint, which is free. Or, you could just use actual envelopes, you know, the way your parents did.

What's the point?

While the Ultimate Goal of using a budget is to get out of debt and build a substantial fortune for retirement, you should also aim to get at least a month's worth of pay saved up in your checking account, just in case you run into any problems with getting paid in the future. By creating a 'buffer,' you eliminate much of the stress that comes with paying bills. If your boss messes up your paycheck, no problem. Bills still get paid on time, because you're using last month's paycheck to cover them.

It may take a few months before you get entirely comfortable using a budget, but don't give up. Once you start clawing back small amounts of money every month and rolling them into your buffer, you'll start to feel like you just got a pay rise. You'll start feeling in control of your finances, and you might even start to see the light at the end of the tunnel.

Here are your basic budgeting steps again, in case you missed one:

1.   Know what you have coming in (paycheck, child support, etc.)

2.   Know what you have going out (bills, spending money, etc.)

3.   Assign every cent to a particular category (Saving, Rent, Utilities, Kids, etc.)

4.   Spend only what you budget for in each category.

5.   If you go over in one category, pull from another, and try harder next month!

6.　　　Save up enough to create a one-month buffer in your checking account, just in case...

7.　　　Don't worry if you don't get it right the first month. Just don't give up!

Now that you've wrapped your mind around telling your money what to do, how about we discuss ways to find more of that money to boss around?

Chapter 5: Why Is Frugal Life Important?

Walking on the path of leading a frugal life, as mentioned in the last chapter, isn't an easy choice to make. But if you want to be the master of your choices, a frugal life is the best teacher to take classes from.

Money saving!

Needless to mention, your hard-earned money is spared the expenditure on things you'd rather avoid. Look around your household and be assured of spotting at least five such items that don't deserve the importance they are given in the form of space in your living room.

Time is money

If you thought it was only money that got saved, think again. Something as precious also made the cut. Yes, time. The best and worst part about time is that it flows. Save your precious hours by following a life of frugality. It goes without saying that when you take your mind off things that you don't need around you, you save yourself a bazillion amount of seconds. Even merely thinking about things that aren't that important consumes hours, depleting your time bank.

Increased management skills

If there's one thing a frugal life teaches a person, it's how to manage in the best hassle-free way possible. Since frugality requires the expenditure of less money and efforts, you get more attention for a narrower range of concerns. These concerns may be humongous in nature but the manner in which you will manage, solve and put them in their respective places would end up increasing your efficient management skills with time and practice.

Become the master of your life

Frugality is also about resisting and making a practice out of it. It's about learning how to say no to lavish expenses and sticking to such decisions. When you do that, you automatically take full control your senses. It is an involuntary reaction of any shopaholic to take out their credit cards upon stumbling across a good discounted shop. Frugal lifestyle, when adopted, would prevent them from doing so by exposing them to the benefits of shaking heads.

Chapter 6: Clothing

Clothing purchases during the year might easily consume an entire financial budget for the typical family or an individual. This is certainly true for families with growing children. Believe me, the kids grow out of those clothes purchase pretty darn fast. Adults require work clothing and leisure clothing. Teens are major clothing hogs. They are really under peer pressured to keep in style. There should be a way to satisfy each member of the family and keep expenses in check. Here are a few ideas to consider. They worked for me. Perhaps, they just might work for you too.

1. Love the smell of new clothing. Buy your new clothing at the end of the season. For example, buy winter clothing at the end of the winter season. Summer threads at the end of the summer. Perhaps, that cute little swimsuit you've had your eye on. Clothing is usually placed on sale at this time. Stores provide extreme discounts during that period. Take advantage of this

opportunity to stock up on wardrobe staples like shirts, jeans, socks, underwear.

2. Extend your wardrobe and money saving power by filling your year round wardrobe with neutral colors that mix and match during the season. Avoid trendy colors like hot pink or passion purple. Remember, just because hot pink is popping this spring, does not suggest that the color is a good fit for your wardrobe. Instead, purchase classic styles in neutral colors that are timeless. Here is a suggestion. Add a few new accessories to give your wardrobe a fresh look.

3. Did you know that you could easily save 50 percent or more by shopping at discount stores? Itis quite true. This is a great way to trim clothing expenses. So, you are really a designer fan. Don't worry, discount stores like Ross and Burlington carry a large number of designer threads. Often, at extreme discounts.

4. I'm all about purchasing clothing with a dual purpose. For example, black slacks are great with a variety jackets, tops, or

shirts. In this circumstance, buy high quality brand clothing because you want them to stand the test of time.

5. Designer clothing for an evening out, cocktail parties, proms, and wedding dresses are available for rent. Forget about spending several hundred dollars on a party dress that you'll only wear once. Rent them out! Check out local retail shops that rent. A local shop in my city rents prom dresses for $49.99 per night. Evening dresses for the same price. Also, inquire at boutiques and smaller clothing stores. Consignment shops, thrift stores, and the Salvation Army are great sources. The Salvation Army reduces prices during the midweek on some clothing. Check them out!

6. This happens frequently. A woman falls in love with a gorgeous outfit at her local department store. However, the outfit is not in her size. Don't buy a size six, if you are a size twelve. More women than you might think practice this. Those outfits usually wind up decorating the clothes

closet for several years, before they are trashed or donated.

7. Avoid those impulse clothing purchases. Take a deep breath before you purchase an item. Ask yourself do you really need those shoes, jeans, dress, or designer scarf. If the answer is yes, pay cash. Hide those credit cards. Nothing stops an impulse buy like handing over cold cash for a purchase.

8. Prepare a clothing list before entering the store. That's right. Don't leave home without it. Never enter the clothing store with a vague idea about purchasing something on sale. Write down your purchases. For example, a new skirt and blouse or pair of work shoes. Search through your wardrobe. Write down the items that you really need. Follow the list to the letter. This should help to curtail some of that impulse buying.

9. Don't hesitant to return an unwanted clothing purchase. Just be prepared to offer a valid reason for returning the item. For example, it does not fit, the wrong

color, or whatever reason. Take it back immediately. Return the item and get your money back or exchange it for something you really like.

10. Don't throw old clothing in the trash. Turn old unwanted clothing into your personal cash cow. Take the clothing and sell it at a local consignment shop or throw a garage sale. You might try selling the good looking stuff on auction sites like eBay. Use the money earned to purchase new clothing or simply save.

11. Frequent thrift shops. Always purchase your used clothing at high end thrift shops. Often, these shops are located in affluent neighborhoods. Many are packed with favorite designer goodies. Don't forget to look around large shopping areas for thrift shops and consignment shops too. Frequently, people donate clothing to shops in affluent neighborhoods. Many pieces donated are still brand-new with tags still attached.

12. Check out the local flea markets, church sales, yard sales, garage sales for

inexpensive finds. These are good sources for a wide variety of clothing to fit the entire family. Browse local newspaper ads on a regular basis to find flea markets or garage sales in your community.

13. Consignment shops are also a cool way to sell old clothing and make some real money. Real value exist in consignment shopping and selling. Give it a try. Don't forget to stop by your local Goodwill and Salvation Army. Bargains galore are at your fingertips. Remember, a large percentage of the donated clothes are new and never worn by the owner. In addition, major retailers donate clothing to thrift shops. One could easily create several outfits for under 100 bucks. Remember, you are getting super bargains and donating to a worthy cause.

14. Start a clothing exchange with a few friends. Ask several to join the fun. Make sure they have similar taste, style and are about the same clothing size. Throw a little get together. Serve a few snacks and drinks. The friends get together and agree

to trade clothing that is similar in value. Great way to obtain a complete new wardrobe for absolutely free. Arrange the clothing exchange parties several times per year.

15. Make your own clothing or re-purpose clothing. Whip out the sewing machine and re-purpose that pair of slacks or jeans. Turn them into a pair of summer shorts. Take that old white t-shirt and dye it a psychedelic color and wear with the re-purposed shorts. Try wearing a dated scarf in an ethnic head wrap, a belt, or a swimsuit cover up.

16. Check the Internet for local sales. Don't forget to scour the Internet for coupons or coupon codes to your favorite retailer. Check daily for coupon codes or clothing coupons to download. These coupons offer a deep discount to free shipping on clothing purchases. It is super easy to find websites offering coupons or coupon codes for Target, Walmart, Macy's, and K-mart.

17. Save on kids clothing. Ask friends and family to donate clothing. Ask family members with children who are about the same age or slightly older to donate clothing that is still in good shape to your family. Lets face facts. Kids out grow their clothing in a few months. Why spend tons of money on clothes that they might wear only a few times. Ask family members to send discarded or outgrown clothing to your family. Let your kids enjoy the clothing for several months. Then donate the clothing to other family members, once your kids outgrow the clothing.

18 Check out Craigslist and Freecycle for clothing that people are giving away for free. Many people list items for free or at a very low cost. You might find a few excellent bargains waiting for you.

19. Mystery Shopping is a fun way to score a few fabulous pieces of clothing. Generally, the mystery shopping service request their members to visit a clothing retailer and purchase clothing. After the visit, they write a detailed report about

the shop. Next, they submit the report along with a valid receipt for the clothing purchase. The company reimburses the mystery shopper for the purchase, plus the shopper earns a few dollars on top of that purchase. Find a legitimate mystery shopping company online and sign up. Caution: Never sign up with a mystery shopping company that insist that you pay them to sign up or for mystery shopping jobs. The company pays you. You do not have to pay for their assignments.

Chapter 7: Frugalism And How Can It Benefit You

Frugality is defined as "sparing" or being economical, especially in relation to money and food. Frugality can be described as the quality of being thrifty. Frugality can be applied to all aspects of your life, not just food and money. This is about looking at all consumables and expenditures. It also involves looking at time. Seeking out areas for improvement. Frugalism involves putting these ideas and concepts into practice.

Frugalism is more than a way to live. It's a way of thinking. Frugalism is a lifestyle many choose to live. It can be used to pay down debt, save money for a big purchase, such as a car or a wedding or to make sure they get the best use of their time and money. Frugality is more than just saving money. It's about living within your means while still enjoying the best of life.

Frugalism has many benefits. Saving money is the number one benefit. There are many benefits to being frugal, beyond just cutting down on some expenses. Frugalism can bring you a new sense of freedom and creativity, as well as a greater appreciation for the environment.

More freedom

Have you ever considered changing your job or retiring earlier? Financial freedom can be achieved by being frugal, so you can take on the risks you've always wanted. You will feel more secure to make those plans for your dream vacation, buy the car you've always wanted, or simply eat out whenever you like. Perhaps you are tired of the constant sales pitches from big corporations that tell you you need their products to survive. You will be able to find other options by being frugalista.

Reducing stress

You can also be more frugal and have less stress in your day. Imagine not worrying about your bills or paying off any debts.

Financial worries are a major cause of stress, according to studies. Everybody wants to live within their means and have enough money for the future. You can realize your dream by being more frugal with your daily decisions. It's possible.

Eco-Friendliness

The environment also benefits from being more frugal. There are many ways to reduce waste and use less. This will not only help you save money, but it also benefits the environment you live in. Although it won't solve all the problems on the planet, it is a good place to start.

More creativity

It's better to repurpose an old piece of furniture than to spend three times the amount on a new one. You can make simple projects around your home that will keep you engaged in creative and constructive endeavors. It also allows you to create the environment you desire. You can find thousands of DYI-friendly projects for pennies. You don't need to rely on the factory designs; you can create your own. This applies to furniture, as well as clothing, accessories, and kitchenware. You will also be able to stay busy and active while you build your new life.

Families with stronger bonds

Every member of the family can contribute to new and innovative ideas about your home and environment. You will discover a new dimension to your family relationships by working together on projects, planning, improvising, and adapting. Everyone can have a voice and encourage one another to find more efficient ways to cut spending.

What makes you a Frugalista

Once you've decided that you want to live a simpler, more relaxed life with less stress, you can start your frugalista lifestyle. It may seem daunting at first, but many people who attempt this have been frustrated by some of the changes required. No matter what your comfort level, go at the pace you are comfortable with. If you don't feel ready, it can cause complete abandonment.

Frugal living is more than just having a few extra cups of coffee or buying a lower-quality deodorant. This is a total overhaul of your entire life. It may seem scary, but it is a great chance to make positive changes in your life. You may have to eat the same breakfast every day for a week. As time passes, you'll no longer view it as a huge sacrifice but as a joyful exercise of discipline.

Create a Plan

It is important to start with a plan. Find a place to sit down and write out your goals. Write down what you want from your life. Be bold and creative. You won't waste money on expensive groceries or huge electric bills.

What has your life been all about? What do you envision yourself doing in the next five, ten, and beyond years? What is your ideal retirement plan? That's it.

You will need to make the next list. It is more challenging. What are your obstacles? How are you spending your money that isn't helping? Here is where honesty and integrity are key. It will be necessary to dig deep into your life and find any areas that are leaking time or money. Do not leave any stone unturned. Take a look at everything, from the food you eat to the shampoo you use. It doesn't matter what it is, put it down on paper.

Identify and remove indulgences you don't need and make a list. Instead of going to Starbucks, you can learn how to make your own coffee or stop drinking coffee altogether. This is one expense that can really add up -- not to mention the fuel and time it takes to get there.

Is it possible for employees to use public transport to get to work. Public transportation not only saves you money on fuel and wear and tear, but it also reduces pollution and traffic. Are you a smoker? Do you smoke cigarettes?

Are you a regular user of lights when you go out of the room? Are you able to downsize your cable TV package or do you still need it? Start thinking creatively and get to work.

The Frugalista Lifestyle:

This new way of living is a challenge. You must accept it as such and be willing to face the challenge. Do not be ashamed or embarrassed by your new lifestyle. It's okay to enjoy it! Show it off and share your accomplishments with others. Do not pay attention to what other people think or say. Smile and say "That's right!" if they call you a cheapie.

You can be your best self by demonstrating determination and discipline. Many believe that more money is the only way to reduce debt and increase savings. You are now realizing that this is not true. You can choose a day and start the challenge. It will last for 30 days. You will see your savings grow and you can keep track of them!

How to Become an Amazing Frugalista

There are many ways to save money, be the best frugalista possible, and still have fun. It's important to have fun while being frugalista. It's not difficult. You can do it!

These are some tips to help you get started.

Prioritize -- Determine if there is a difference between needs and wants. You can divide the page vertically by using a notebook. Place the date of the day at the top. Next, label the columns "Wants" or "Needs". Start listing what you are most likely to buy. You will find that many of your needs are just desires you can live with.

* Stop spending -- This tip may seem silly, but it is vital. Pay attention to how often your hand is in your wallet, purse, or pocket. Pay attention to your urges to buy. Many people think that a dollar is enough. However, each dollar adds up. Don't take money with you when you go out. Don't take your card with you. You should only

take enough cash if you're going to purchase something absolutely essential.

Reduce your debt. As you work through this process, you'll find that you have less need of plastic and will want it less. Reduce the interest rate on the lowest-interesting credit card and save the rest. Contact the credit card companies if you have debt. Tell them what you're doing. Tell them that you are serious about paying off your credit card debt. They may be able to waive interest fees in order to help you pay off your debt. If you find something that is significant, you can put it on your wish list. You can then use cash later to pay it. You will get the money, don't worry!

* The library is a great place to be -- It's one of the best places in any city. You can find almost anything you need for entertainment or news, and they are completely free. Take a library card to see all the great things the library has. The library offers books, movies, newspapers, and many other activities for children.

Many libraries provide free Internet access, so you can check your emails and stay in touch with your friends via social media. You can also use the library's resources to save time when you aren't at home operating your lights or electrical appliances such as televisions and computers. Easy access to libraries is possible because most are located along bus routes.

* Get a green thumb -- It all depends on where you live and when you begin your frugal lifestyle. It is a great way to save money, reduce waste, and eat a healthier diet. You don't need a lot of space or you are new to gardening. Start with vegetables that are easy to grow. You can find information at the library about gardening techniques and the best crops for your area. Because they can grow almost anywhere, tomatoes are very easy to grow and maintain. Another thing that is easy to grow is herbs. They take up very little space. You can also grow your own herbs to add flavor and color to your budget-friendly dishes.

Sharpen your scissors and clip those coupons! You can find rebates and freebies in the Sunday paper. For sale dates and buy one-get-one deals, check the Sunday paper. Stock up on good deals and take advantage of discount points and reward points.

* Do not let others do what you can do for you. Being self-sufficient is something to aim for. You can cut your hair and change your oil yourself, as well as do small repairs around your home. Before you hire someone to do something, make sure you do it yourself. There are many books and cookbooks that can help you, as well as repair guides. You just need to approach each task with patience, confidence, and the belief that you can accomplish it. Frugality doesn't just mean saving money. It also means taking control of your life. You can accomplish anything anyone can, even if it takes you a bit longer to do it.

* Buy secondhand -- Don't buy anything new (within reason). Use thrift shops, estate sales, estate sales, secondhand

stores and thrift stores to your advantage. You can save a lot of money by learning how to fix or mending your product.

* Save energy -- Turn off the switch! How many times have you moved from one room into another without switching off the lights? Be aware of how much electricity you use. Unplug appliances and turn off lights that aren't being used. You can save energy by investing in lightbulbs that are energy-efficient and taking advantage of daylight hours for household chores. Cold water is best for washing clothes. It saves water heaters from working too hard, and the clothes will still be clean. Line-dry your clothes instead of drying them with an electric dryer. You can have a family camping out in one room, so that only one electric fan is on during the summer heat. You will notice a significant difference in your next bill if you do your research.

* No to dining out! STAY IN! Eating out can be expensive, especially if you tip well and add a few drinks. Invite friends to dinner

and drink. Each friend will be given a course (appetizers, desserts, etc.). This is a great way to save money while still enjoying your social life. You can all enjoy a wonderful dinner together while you prepare the main course. It will cost you less than going out for dinner. For great savings, try our organic recipes.

Restaurants can charge you to prepare and serve the same food as you make at home, which can lead to a significant increase in their profits. It is important to plan your meals and shop smartly. Don't get caught in a situation where you don't have a plan for preparing a meal. This can lead to a financial disaster. Learn how to pack lunches for work and school. You can carry a water container with you.

* Don't go to the movies. It is costly. A home movie marathon is a great way of saving money. Grab your movie candy from the dollar store and grab some popcorn. Then, relax on your couch. Here are some ways to save money on rental costs. Redbox allows you to rent movies.

You can rent a good selection of movies starting at $1 per night.

Get a board to keep you entertained! Entertainment doesn't need to be expensive. There are many ways to keep your family entertained without spending a lot. Puzzles and board games are great ways to keep everyone entertained for hours. It's fun and easy to spend time with friends while having great conversations. You can organize a "potluck" dinner with other families in your area where everyone brings something to share. For entertainment, you could play sports, cards, or parlor games.

* Group errands can be done -- It is easier to save time and fuel by doing all your errands on one trip instead of spreading them across several trips. Pick a day for bills payment, grocery shopping, and returning library books.

* Get rid of your car - This is especially important if you have multiple cars. You can walk, bike, take public transport, or use Zipcar to share your car. Try it out for

a month to see how much money you can save.

* Exercise - Protecting our health is the best way to save money. Regular exercise can boost your immune system and keep your muscles healthy. It also releases endorphins which make you happy. Get outside and get your exercise. You won't be distracted by the television and endless stream of advertisements for products you don't need.

*Repair instead of replacing - Instead of buying new clothing, repair it. A simple patch or seam repair can bring years of life to garments that would otherwise be discarded. Are you unable to sew? You can trade babysitting and dog walking with someone who can. You can also trade tips about how to save money together! Another money-saving tip is to repair appliances rather than replacing them. While you may want a top-of the-line refrigerator, it is more cost-effective to have your fridge repaired first. You'll save a lot if you can get $200 worth of repairs to keep your fridge running for another five years.

Chapter 8: Streaming Services

This section encompasses any streaming service with a monthly fee. This includes Netflix, Hulu, YouTube Red, Disney+, HBO Max, and any other video subscription. The tips in this section will also work for music subscriptions like Pandora, Spotify, Amazon Music Unlimited, or whichever music subscription you use.

The first thing to ask yourself is which streaming services do you pay for? Make a list and put the monthly amount you pay for these services. Sometimes it will shock you to see that you are spending a hundred dollars or more on these. Second thing you should do is ask yourself if you really need all these services. Do you pay for Sirius Radio when you have Spotify and Bluetooth in your car? If that's the case, can you live without Sirius Radio? Did you start paying for HBO because you wanted to watch Game of Thrones but never got around to it? Be honest with yourself and cancel the services you don't need, because every month you pay for it without using it is money wasted. Stop putting it off, because 9 out of 10 times it will take less than 10 minutes on the phone or online to cancel the service.

So, you made a list of the services you use and you decided that you can't eliminate any of them. The good news is that there are still ways to save! If you are living with roommates or with family, then ask the other people in the household if they pay for the same service. I was shocked to find that my three siblings were all individually paying for Netflix but lived in the same house. I told them to cancel two of the services and get a family plan on the remaining account. This way they could just share the password. Under Netflix regulations this is allowed, as long as the members are living in the same household.

You guessed it… time to crunch the numbers!

Three members under the same household paying for Netflix. Currently the cheapest Netflix subscription is $8.99 and allows you to use Netflix on one screen at standard definition quality. Meanwhile, the premium account costs $15.99, gives you access to HD and Ultra HD, and allows up to four screens at the same time. There's also a "medium" option that allows two screens, but since there were three members we went with the premium.

They were paying $8.99 x 3 = $26.97 per month x 12 = $323.64 per year

After the change: One person paying $15.99 per month x 12 = $191.88 per year

At the end, my siblings got one extra screen access, HD and Ultra HD quality video, and saved $130 in the first year of making the change. If you make this change, you can go ahead and split the cost with your roommates or family members.

If there are only two of you, then you can still save by getting the plan in the middle. Not only that, but you would also upgrade to HD quality. Let's take a look.

Separate Netflix for two: $8.99 x 2 = $17.98 per month x 12 = $215.76 per year

Family plan Netflix for two: One person paying $12.99 per month x 12 = $155.88 per year

The savings aren't as high, but you'd still be saving $59.88 throughout the year and would upgrade to HD quality.

Honestly, switching my siblings to the Netflix family plan wasn't the only change I made for them. I started asking them more about other services they paid for and found the following. Along with the three of them paying Netflix separately, one of them was paying for Spotify while the other two used free music-streaming services, and one paid for Hulu with ads.

Netflix: $8.99 x 3 = $26.97/mth

Spotify: $9.99 x 1 = $9.99/mth

Hulu: $5.99 x 1 = $5.99/mth

Spending before changes: $26.97 + $9.99 + $5.99 = $42.95/mth x 12 months = $515.40

I convinced them to each pay for one family plan, which split the costs pretty evenly. These are the numbers after making the changes:

Netflix: $15.99 x 1 = $15.99/mth

Spotify: $9.99 x 1 = $14.99/mth

Hulu: $11.99 x 1 = $14.99/mth

Spending after changes: $15.99 + $14.99 + $14.99 = $45.97/mth x 12 months = $551.64

This means that all three of them upgraded to unlimited, ad-free music and Netflix, and gained access to Hulu without ads for only $2 more per month. As an added bonus, since Spotify comes with access for up to 6 accounts, my brother's fiancé and my mom also got access to unlimited music with no ads (again, they all live under the same household). They all got an upgrade on services they actually use on a regular basis. If you are living under the same household and find a way to share costs, oftentimes you can save money by going with the family plan. It definitely worked out for my family, who are all happy with the changes made.

Let's look at other ways to save. Remember that most of these services have a free month for new customers who want to try it out. Netflix is nice enough to send you an email reminding you that your free month is coming to an end, but other companies just roll you into their monthly plan. If you forget and are charged for the month, just call them up to cancel the account and ask for a refund for that month (if it's only been a few days after the charge). Every time I've done that it has worked for me. Another option is downgrading to the service's cheaper or free option. You might find that watching or listening to the commercials is worth the money you're saving every month.

Chapter 9: Food/Groceries

Take control of the money you spend on weekly groceries with the following tips. I know one clever gal who was spending about $800 bucks a month on food. This was a bit extreme for a single woman. She used a few ideas like the following to reduce her spending by half.

Dining Out. Avoid dinning out at expensive restaurants. Perhaps, limit to once a month or special occasions. Start packing a lunch and taking it to work. Stay away from those snack machines at work. Avoid fast foods at all cost. They can really take a bite out of your wallet.

Supermarkets. Supermarkets are set up to make you buy impulse foods. Always create a grocery list before hitting the store. Check your fridge and cupboards. Write down the items that you really need to restock. Stick to the items on the list and avoid those impulse purchases.

Plan Menus. Sit down every week and create a menu for the entire week. Plan weekly menu's for the entire month. Write down the items that are required to create the menus. Add these to your grocery list. This is one way to make sure that you only purchase the food items that you really require.

Weekly Budget. Create a weekly budget for grocery shopping and stick to the budget. Those who create a weekly budget are more aware of how they spend their money and keep control on the spending. Take along a calculator and keep tabs on how much you are spending on the items. When you get close to your budget limit, stop shopping!

Cut Back. Another way to easily cut back on grocery spending is to reduce the amount of meat that you buy. Instead try replacing those heavy meaty meals with frozen veggies instead.

Scraps. Never throw away those scraps or leftovers. Get in the habit of building meals around those leftovers. Leftover meatloaf and roast beef makes great sandwiches. Take left over veggies and make a nice thick veggie soup dish.

Freeze. Get in the habit of cooking large meals and freezing them. Place them in freezer bags and store in the freezer for multiple meals at a later time.

Food Coupons. A lot of people think coupon clipping is a waste of time. The real deal is that clipping food coupons might save the average shopper a hundred dollars or more per month. I've saved as much as $50 bucks on one trip to the grocery store with coupons dowloaded from Couponmom.com.

Food Saver Cards. Sign up with grocery stores and join their food saver club. The store issues you a money saving card that is scanned at the checkout. On average, you could save anywhere from about 10% and up simply by presenting your food saver club card.

Shop When Full. Never shop when you are hungry. Studies show that people who grocery shopping when they are hungry tend to buy more junk food. If your feel hunger pangs, eat something. It is better to shop for your groceries on a full stomach to stop impulse purchases.

Weekly Specials. Scan your newspapers or go online and search for weekly specials at your local super-market. Look around the store for those hidden unadvertised specials. Remember to only purchase the item, if it is something that you truly need.

Forget Brand Loyalty. Name brand items might cost considerably more than the store brand or off brand product. Honestly, think about it for a second. Is there really that much difference between a name brand can of green beans or the store brand? What about that expensive butter, tomato sauce, or sugar. The fact is that many store brands are actually made by the name brand companies and labeled differently.

Favorites. If you see your favorite brand on sale, make sure that you stock up on the item wisely. For example, if your usual Ketchup is 2.99 per bottle and you see it on sale for 99 cents, stock up and buy three bottles of the item.

Avoid Prepackaged Foods. Avoid prepackaged foods as much as possible. Learn to cook from scratch. Use your culinary skills to make your own cakes and pastries. Bake your own pies, pizza to save money.

Junk Food. Junk food is too expensive and waste your money. There is a reason why it is called junk food. It has zero nutritional value and is making you fat. Instead buy fresh fruits and vegetables. Avoid those sugary sweet processed drinks and sodas. They contain zero nutritional value and they are very expensive per ounce served. Instead drink water or make a large pitcher of fresh tea in the summer to soothe thirst.

Grow Your Own. Ever think about growing your own vegetables and fruits? This is easy, if you live in a rural area or own a yard. Even a small patio might provide enough space to grow vegetables. City dwellers should consider joining a gardening group that grows their own vegetables and fruits in the summer and share the bounty. This is a way to get free fresh nutritious veggies and fruits. The only cost is your hard work and taking care of the garden.

Share, Share restaurant meals to save. t restaurant meals are large enough to split between two people. Or you could dine out at a less expensive restaurant with coupons for special meals. This is another way to save big and still get to dine out occasionally even on a budget.

Group Meals. Invite friends over for a group dinner. Invite several friends over every week or more often. Each friend brings a food item to share with the group. For example, one friend might make the dessert, another makes a main course meal, others vegetable dishes. Everyone gets to enjoy a large variety of foods and save money.

Chapter 10: How To Get Stuff For Free

Yes, you can sometimes get the stuff you need for absolutely nothing. There are a couple places to check. Freecycle.org is a site where people post stuff they no longer want and are trying to give away. It isn't uncommon to see stuff on there that's in pretty good shape. Sign up using your Yahoo account and choose the metro area closest to where you live to start browsing the free stuff. You can find everything from clothes to furniture on there, so keep an eye peeled for items you can use.

Another place to check is Craigslist. Go to the metro area closest to you and click on "free" in the for sale listings. If you don't find what you're looking for, try expanding out to nearby areas. A quick check of the area I live in revealed the following items for free:

• River rock

- A kitten

- Children's DVDs

- A walker

- A 56-inch TV

- A decorative palm tree

- Two boats

- Moving boxes

- Treadmill

- A Fushigi ball

- A brown leather couch (in good condition)

- Wood garage door

This is just a small sample of the type of stuff you can find for free on Craigslist. Keep your eyes peeled for stuff you can use.

Free Samples

There are a number of place you can get free samples of your favorite products. Thefreesite.com is a directory that lists a ton of free stuff you can get from manufacturers. There's enough on the site to keep you busy for hours.

Another place to check is your favorite retailers website. Sites like Krogers and Walmart have free samples sections that offer free samples of groceries and household items.

If you have a product you particularly like or want to try, contact the manufacturer directly. My husband recently wrote a popular weight lifting supplement company to find out what they recommended he take to help lose weight and put on muscle. They responded by asking for his address and they sent out over a hundred dollars worth of free supplements. I was shocked when we opened the large box to find four full-size containers of supplements.

Free or Cheaper Long Distance Calls

If you make a lot of long-distance calls and have huge phone bills, there are a couple options you can use to really cut down the bill.

The first is Skype. Sign up at skype.com and have the people you call long-distance a lot sign up too. As long as the two of you are using Skype via the Internet, the calls are completely free. You can make free video calls or regular calls. If you want to call people who aren't on Skype, the fees are much cheaper than normal long-distance providers.

Another option is to get an Xbox 360 and sign up for Xbox Live. This allows you to chat with your long-distance friends via Live. While this service is intended to allow gamers to chat with one another while they play video games online, there's nothing stopping you from logging on and talking without playing games. It costs $50 a year to sign up for Xbox Live and you can talk to anyone in the world that has a high-speed connection and an Xbox.

Scratch and Dent Stores

If your area has stores where scratched or dented goods are sold, you can save a lot of money by shopping these places.

I'm lucky to have a dented canned goods store right down the street from me. When I need canned foods like soups and vegetables, I always check there first. I'm rarely disappointed and usually get the food I need for around half what it costs at the supermarket. These stores typically stock more than just canned goods—they also sell overstock items from other stores and other food items with damaged packages.

When buying canned goods from a scratch and dent store, it's important to examine the cans you're buying closely. Look for leaks or for the top or bottom to be puffed out—this indicates the food inside has gone bad. Be sure to check the expiration date. I've purchased canned goods and took them home, only to find they were well past the expiration date.

Check these stores frequently in order to get the best deals. Stock is constantly rotating and you never know what you're going to find. They buy truck loads of stuff and are constantly putting new stuff out.

If you're in the market for new furniture or appliances, check around to see if there's a scratch and dent store that sells appliances or furniture near you. Sears has a number of scratch and dent stores spread across the U.S. There are also specialty stores that buy scratched and dented items for cheap and resell them.

As long as you don't mind a minor flaw or two, you can sometimes get hundreds of dollars off the retail price. These items usually come with a full warranty, so it's just like buying a brand new item.

Drink More, Save More

Now that I've got your attention, let me tell you what I'm talking about. I'm talking about water. Drink more water to save more money.

Here's how. It's recommended you drink 8 to 10 glasses of water a day. That's 8 to 10 less glasses of juice, milk, soda and beer you'll be drinking. This will allow you to save the money you'd normally spend on those items. I've managed to completely cut soda out of my daily diet and rarely drink juices and beer. I still drink a couple glasses of milk a day, but that's a lot healthier than the other options.

If you don't like water, try sprucing it up a bit with a wedge of lemon, orange or lime or a slice of cucumber. I usually ask for lemon water when I'm at a restaurant. They're more than willing to accommodate this request and you save the money drinks would have cost.

If you drink a big glass of water before you eat a meal, you're going to suppress your appetite and help with digestion. You'll save money on your food bill because you'll eat less and you'll feel healthier because you'll be properly hydrated.

Chapter 11: Use Solar Energy To Save Money

Solar energy is a great way to save money and live efficiently. Solar panels are cheap and easy to install and some companies are providing a step by step DIY (Do it yourself) kit to install solar panels on your roof or any space where exposure to sunlight is essential. These kits are cheap and easy to install and saves you a lot of money and energy. Electricity is becoming more and more expensive and the amount you spend per unit is much higher as compared to the amount you spend on installing solar panels. Some electronic devices of your home life tube lights, CFLs, fans, etc. can easily run on solar power, thereby cutting your electricity bill cost.

I have seen many innovative ways to save money through the use of solar energy and you can also invent your own way. Alkaline batteries and cells that you buy from the market are also very expensive and you have to minimize their use by using solar energy. Solar chargers for your batteries, mobile phones, and digital cameras cut down the electricity bill as well as extend the life of your batteries. Some solar chargers are so compact that you can take them with you while going for an outing and listen to your favourite songs on MP3 without any interruption.

Solar powered flashlights and calculators are a great example of electronic devices that save money and work efficiently without the need to replace the batteries often. Whenever you go to buy these electronics, then look for the solar powered version because you can use them for a long time without interruption thereby saving a lot of money on battery replacement.

Enter Some Sweepstakes to Win and Save Money

You can save a big amount of money or win some great prizes by entering into the sweepstakes. There are many promotions and contests available on the internet or newspapers that can give you an opportunity to win big or earn some money. Many things have really changed today in sweepstakes since the days of mail-in only entry, now a person can simply enter his information online to win some big sweepstakes. But remember that everything that glitters is not gold and cross check the authenticity of sweepstakes before you enter your secret information like your credit card details. Check twice if any sweepstake company is asking you to pay some amount in advance and pay only if you make sure that they are genuine.

Applying to every sweepstake on the internet sometimes becomes very daunting and you have to type your information on the forms every time. You can get rid of this conundrum by simply automatic form fillers like Roboform to save your time and ease the process of filling your information. The best way to level the playing field and increase your opportunities of winning will be to determine a comprehensive site that both lists and tracks your entries. There are many genuine websites like www.Online-sweepstakes.com and www.Sweepsadvantage.com that should provide you updated information about the sweepstakes in your area or on the internet. So, sign up on these websites and increase your chances to grab the sweepstakes, some personal blogs are already available to you that can also provide you the directory of companies that arrange sweepstakes.

Winning sweepstakes is a long and time consuming process and you have to keep patience before you finally win one. I had won a sweepstake after making some efforts for around 6 months, but don't worry because many sweepstakes can really bring you a big win.

Find and Claim Unclaimed Property

Do you know something about unclaimed property? There are many bank accounts, lands, old bond certificates that is still unclaimed and you can easily claim them. You would have seen many TV commercials and online banner ads that will offer to find this unclaimed property for you for a small fee, but the truth is that you can find and claim it for free. If you are living in America, then you can find the official website of most treasure offices on the internet, where you can find unclaimed property. However, finding a property is a bit time consuming, especially if you have lived in various states. Some of the best websites where you can easily find the unclaimed properties are missingmoney.com and unclaimed.org. These websites are official and maintained by NAUPA (National Association of Unclaimed Property Administration). Many search tools are available at these sites so that you can easily find unclaimed properties easily.

The easy way to find unclaimed property with your name is to go to the website missingmoney.com, then enter your first name, last name, and state of residence. The database will find a match for you. Now, you can either claim money online providing the required documents, or claim the money via mail by filling out the claim form and notarizing by a notary public. Instructions vary in different states, so search for the procedure for your state. Look for the rules and regulations for how to claim the unclaimed property if you are living in a different country than America, because all countries have different laws regarding how to claim an unclaimed property.

Take Degrees in Off Season to Save Money

You can actually save up to 50% on the cost of your tuition by taking them on off season. Many colleges, especially community and non-traditional will provide you a huge discount if you enrol in the off peak season. These classes are organized during very late evening meetings, or during holidays.

You can check with your admissions office, whether they provide any discount for less popular time slots, and be prepared to join the classes in some odd timing. Once you are confirmed that these classes will be discounted, ensure your seat by enrolling early. Many online courses are also available that provides you discount during off peak season, so search for some online degree programs with discount in off peak season.

Chapter 12: How To Create Frugal Meals

Now it's time to learn about how to create your very own frugal meals that will save you time, headache, and of course money. There are many ways that you can save money by creating your own frugal meals and should be planned out each week to ensure that you are living the true frugal lifestyle and creating more money in your pocket as well. Here are a few tips and suggestions to changing you and your families eating habits into a delicious and creative "frugal" lifestyle!

Cutting down Prices on Meats – with the price of meats at your grocers at an all-time high, many people find themselves dreading to go through the meat isle of your local grocery store. Realize that it doesn't always have to be that way and you can come off getting a cheaper rate when you purchase your meats in bulk. Everyone knows you can't simply purchase tons of meat and eat it all in time before it goes bad, which is why it is a good idea to have a deep freezer to store their extra meat not being used at the time.

Having a deep freezer to store extra meats allows you do by larger quantities of meat and store the portions that you won't be using at that time, which saves you a ton of money in the end. Buying in bulk really is a great way to save you money each month on food products. Hamburger meat is of course the cheapest meat that you can purchase and you can buy them by the pounds at a cheaper rate in comparison to other meats. There are tons of meal ideas when it comes to hamburger meat and is your best option when it comes to purchasing meats "frugally." So make sure the next time you are shopping frugally in your grocery store that you choose to buy in bulk at the meat department and you will see how much money you can save at the end of each month by using this money saving method!

Grow Your Own Garden – This is a great way to cut down on your costs when it comes to purchasing vegetables. Making a garden is not a hard task at all and can also help you through the winter months, if you make a big enough garden. You can literally buy seeds, soil, and start tilling your way to savings that you never imagined! Many of your own home grown vegetables are tastier in my opinion than store bought produce anyways.

When you take in effect of how much vegetable seeds cost you as well as the soil needed to help your garden grow, you truly are making a great savings and vegetables that can last you all year round. No more spending gobs and gobs of money buying vegetables at the super market, you now can save all of that money and eat your own homegrown vegetables. You can also deep freeze the vegetables that you won't be using, then when you are running low you simply go to your deep freeze and pull out a ton more food for both you and your family.

This is a BIG-TIME money saver and a great way to start living frugally...trust me!

Use Leftovers as Much As Possible – this method is really great for larger families! Using leftovers can come in quite handy when it comes to saving money on meals! Try creating meals that you can store in your freezers or for the next day for lunch or dinner. You can easily create two pots filled with delicious spaghetti and freeze the portions that you and your family have not consumed to eat them at a later date. You are literally making your own convenient meals...without of course paying what you would normally pay for a convenience meal. You can also create chili and save the leftovers for a later date in the same manner. This is a mega money saver! You can also pre make bigger quantities of other foods or meals and freeze them to set for a later date!

Many people also find that cooking a turkey or ham and then slicing it up to make different meals is a big time money saver. Think about all of the many things you could literally make turkey and ham out of... you could literally slice it all up and make your very own sandwich meat, or even make various different meals such as turkey salad. You can research and find other tips and ideas with leftovers online to help you with saving both time and money, while at the same time giving you delicious recipe ideas that you can use to spread your meals out and make more out of your meals!

Create Your Own Desserts vs. Expensive Premade Desserts – Alright Betty Crocker, it's time for you to pull out your oven mitt and your apron... it's time to make your very own inexpensive desserts that the whole family will love! It is proven that created your own homemade food items will save you a ton of cash and this is no different with pastries or desserts! In fact you can even live "frugally" by baking your very own bread. The reason why it is so cheap to create your own desserts is because the ingredients that you use can be bought in mass quantity and are very inexpensive to purchase. Rather than going out and purchasing an already premade dessert why not save tons of money following your favorite recipe book and creating your own "frugal" desserts! This is another great way for you to save money that you can literally see at the end of the month!

There are tons of different recipes online that you can find that will help you create your very own "frugal" meals that your entire family will love! Make sure that you keep everyday spices in stock as well as flour. You will be surprised out how easy it really can be to save money eating the "frugal" way... don't just take my word for it... find out for yourself!

Chapter 13: Frugalism And Fashion Tips

Being a frugalista doesn't mean you have to sacrifice looking amazing. On the contrary, it gives you more freedom to create a new look! There are several shopping alternatives when it comes to fashion that can save you money and still keep the admiring stares on you.

• Take inventory of your closet — The first thing you would want to do is to take inventory of your closet. Determine what you actually wear and what you don't. Statistics say that people wear only 20 percent of what is in their closet. By doing this, you will be able to see what exactly you prefer to wear when it comes to fashion.

• Look for your personal "classics" — Figure out the styles that you feel most comfortable with. Dressing as neutral as possible will help you stay in style and keep your pocket full. Staying away from the obviously crazy fads that won't last long is the best route to take.

• Always be on the lookout for sales — Watch for sales or discounted clothing. Take advantage of coupons for both clothing and accessories. This is especially good with children's shoes. There is no need to buy them expensive shoes since they grow so fast. Many times you can get two pairs of shoes at a discount. If you are buying for a child, get one pair that fits now and one pair that's a little larger to grow into.

• Sew your buttons — Learning to sew is certainly a challenge that requires dedication and patience, but it will open a door to fashion freedom. Repairing, mending, or making the alterations yourself instead of buying new clothes will save a lot of money. You can update last year's wardrobe to reflect the latest styles. Just visit the library and browse the latest fashion magazines. In time, you could learn to make your own clothes from a pattern and dress your children in the latest mall fashions for a fraction of the cost.

• Get thrifty — Check out consignment, vintage, and thrift stores (and even flea markets) for not only regular clothing, but accessories as well. Many times they may just need a little mending and a good washing and they will look good as new. Most thrift stores have set prices for entire racks of clothing and some even run specials on certain days. Hats, belts, shoes, and kids' clothes can all be purchased at thrift and consignment shops for very little cash.

• Lose the label — Name-brand clothes are expensive. If you cannot find what you want in the secondhand store, try discount boutiques or factory outlet stores that carry damaged or misprinted goods. Those are great places to pick up items like socks and underwear that you wouldn't buy secondhand. Do your homework and look around.

• Mix and match — Invest in the basics. Choose certain articles of clothing and accessories that can be matched with many different outfits. Colors like black, brown, and white are versatile and can normally fit into many style ensembles. Jeans work wonders as everyday wear and a single pair of jeans can match hundreds of different tops, blouses, jackets, and the like.

• Buy during off seasons — Buying clothes at the end of the season when they are discounted is a great way to be ready for next year. Things like heavy shirts for the kids, winter coats, and boots can all be purchased at clearance prices when the weather breaks. Similarly, the end of summer is the perfect time to get ready for next year's pool party or picnic.

One of the best tips for fashion and being frugal with clothing is proper care. Taking the extra effort to keep your clothing nice makes them last for a long time. As mentioned above, wash in cold water to protect colors and hang dry. And only wash when it's necessary. Over-washing not only wastes water and power, but can damage clothes and make them fade.

Frugalism and Interior Design Ideas and Tips

Sprucing up your home doesn't have to be costly. Learning to do many things on your own can save a lot of money and be a great way to get the whole family involved in a project. Simply clearing away clutter and putting a fresh coat of paint can brighten up a space and make it look more inviting.

• Keeping your home clean and sparkling! — This may not seem like the most fun way to decorate, but it really makes a difference. Washing floors, vacuuming, and keeping the windows clean to let in sunlight will brighten up any room. It's free and you will be amazed at how much difference a good spring cleaning will make.

• Open space is refreshing — Many make the mistake of looking for things to fill up spaces that would look just fine — if not better — being left free of clutter or any decoration. Think about what you are planning to buy and see if you can make it cheaper.

• Keep your decorating simple — Don't overdo it. Too many decorations can spoil the atmosphere and ruin the mood of your room. Create a point of focus with one or two well-placed items.

• Do it yourself — Simple homemade decorations made with a glue gun and supplies from a craft store can solve many design dilemmas. Table centerpieces, wall decor, and holiday furnishings can all be made easily with little effort. When you spot an idea in a magazine or while window-shopping, see if you can duplicate it. The library has many books about crafts and designs that you can do at home.

• Get creative — As for new curtains, you can visit a fabric store and choose from hundreds of different styles or patterns and then sew and hem them on your own. You can also create window treatments from old clothes, sheets, or dresses that you find in the thrift store. Hanging simple dinner plates on the wall can add zest any room. You can find different styles and patterns at the thrift store or maybe you have some in a box somewhere. Mix and match different styles and create a mural to break up the monotony of a solid wall.

Another way to liven up a blank wall is to hang tapestries or decorative cloth from wooden dowels. You can even create an accent wall by painting it a different shade than the rest. This is an inexpensive way to offset the monotony in a space.

• Say yes to secondhand pieces — Buying secondhand furniture or watching the trash is a good way to find quality item that may just need a little care. Wood furniture can be stripped, sanded, and re-varnished usually in a few days. Check out the hardware store to find the right color stain or even new knobs or handles for dressers or end tables. No one will believe when you tell them this beautiful end table was once sitting on the curb.

• Frame it — Frames can be bought inexpensively and you can even print out pictures, Japanese symbols, or even make your own prints! Put them in a frame and hang them. This can also be done with cartoon characters for the kids' room.

• Spruce up your kitchen and bath — Ceramic paint in the kitchen or bath can put a fresh look on old tiles. Hardware stores sell all types of shiny knobs and handles that can be replaced on cabinet doors and drawers for very little cost.

Chapter 14: What You Can Do

Now kindle and MOOCs are where you get the information, and here is where you use it to make money. There are a number of freelancer or micro job sites, like Fiverr and Upwork. These two have been around longer than most, but they are not the only ones. There are many freelancer sites like Guru, Microworkers, SEOclerks, and People Per Hour. Check them out and see what you think. I would apply for more than one as there is a lot of competition out there. Take your pick they all do the same thing. You have to find a site where you can sell your skill set. I think the most profitable marketable skill is something that helps other people make money. At the moment the hottest thing in cyberspace is Facebook advertisements, soon to be overtaken by Linkedin advertisements. These are pay per click similar to google adwords but they are new. Linkedin adwords is so new very few people know how to do it. So if you have mastered Linkedin adwords you can write your own ticket. But you must be able to produce results. If you don't or can't you will be pushed aside by someone who can and if you are helping people make money, you should get a better hourly rate.

Now when you are dealing worldwide on a 24 hour basis, the world's cheapest salary is the bottom rate. And you will find some payments quoted, are ridiculous but, someone in Asia or the old Eastern Bloc will think they are the best salary ever. So some things you can forget about like writing articles or ebooks or ghost writing. At $1 a 100 words and up to $3 a 100, you have to be either desperate, or living in some back water village in Vietnam or Croatia or someplace like that. Unless you can type one hundred words per minute and then you still have to research the topic. But then again, if you can put together a sales page that makes money, your payment goes way up. The specialist skills are what brings in the money. So before you spend hours learning a new skill and setting yourself up, make sure the skill is in demand and the salary range is worth it. I first heard this from Dan Kennedy from Magnetic Marketing fame, whether he was the first to say it or not, I don't know. "It took me five years to become an overnight success." And that is not far wrong. As you will find out very soon, when you start marketing yourself on freelancer sites or blog sites or where ever you choose to make some extra money.

If you want to try freelancing then read everything on the sites, especially the free pdf download about how to set up to get seen. As that is a big problem, getting noticed and then apply for everything you can that is listed on your profile. And just get something to put on your profile. Check out kindle and see if they have a cheap book on freelancing just to get you started. To survive living cheap you have to learn new skills, and the sooner you learn the new skill, the sooner you can start using it. And it is always better to learn from somebody who has mastered the skill, than trial and error which is a very slow way of doing things.

One of the biggest rages at the moment is self publishing on kindle. But just remember, it takes five years to become an overnight success. So the more learning you do from the masters, the shorter the five years gets. And to survive you have to shorten the five years. That is where kindle comes in. Read everything you can on what you are learning. The sooner you master it, the sooner you will profit from what you have learned. Publishing on kindle is a lot of learning, but be thankful many authors have already done it and written about it. So read up on what they did and do it. I don't know how long kindle will be the rage, and publishing on kindle is very easy. But making money from selling books is not. So if you want to go that route, start reading and doing.

Always follow the money. And to learn a new topic is getting cheaper with kindle. You can read three to six books, and you will be very clued up on a new idea to make money, for less than $30. Then again the people who read the most books and are good at teaching, make the most money. Tony Robbins has read nearly every book on personal development, and tried out what they said and now look at him. The key is reading the book then doing what the book suggests. The more times you do this, the more you will learn and know what works and what doesn't.

Chapter 15: First Person: Why I Live On A Budget

Although I'm an accountant, I confess — I'm horrible without a budget. Basically, if I have $20 in my pocket, I spend it. If I have $200, I'll spend that, too. It's not something I'm proud of. It's just the cold, hard truth. That's why I put myself on a budget years ago and I'll never live without one.

• Weekly Expenses

I break my budget into sections — depending on how frequent the expense and it all goes on one nice, tidy spreadsheet. Gas and groceries are weekly expenses. But, I also budget my lunch and spending money. I give myself a certain amount each week for each expense and when it's gone, it's gone — it's that simple.

• Monthly Expenses

My monthly expenses are a little more involved. Everything goes on the spreadsheet – phone, cable, car payments, mortgage, and electric – even charity contributions. If I pay for the expense on a monthly basis, it goes in the monthly section and those monies are set aside with each paycheck for that purpose and that purpose only.

• Yearly Expenses

I used to struggle with large, yearly bills like car insurance, homeowners insurance and life insurance – which all seemed to come in the same week. Now I just divide the amount by 12 and set aside money for those bills – just like any other monthly bill. This works like a charm.

• Reserves

Over the years, I found one of my biggest problems were what I called my "surprise" bills. Now, what's funny is that they really shouldn't have come as a surprise, because I knew (eventually) I'd have to spend money on these items. I guess the real surprise was that I never seemed to be prepared when I was faced with the actual expense.

But, then I got smart and I started funding what I now call my "reserves." I have reserves for everything from emergency vet bills and health care deductibles to home repairs and birthday presents. You name it, I probably reserve for it. I treat it like a yearly bill. I may not know when it's coming – but, I know it's coming and budgeting for those expenses means I'll have the money I need when the expense finally comes along.

As you can see, I'm serious about my budget. I don't rob from Peter to pay Paul. I've been there, done that – it didn't work for me. What works is a good, old-fashioned, detailed budget and an iron-clad will to follow it. Now, if I would just start budgeting my time the same way, I would probably get a lot more done.

Chapter 16: Smart Tips To Make A Great Budget

Now that we have covered the basics where it comes to preparing that budget of ours, let's take a look at some of the tips that will ensure that we really do a great job at it, after all, and that the whole purpose of making that budget in the very first place, that of spending less than what we earn, is firmly etched into our mind.

• Know the amount of money you are 'actually' making. We have already discussed in the earlier chapter the importance of arriving at that 'average monthly figure' that will be used for the purposes of budgeting. However, it is important to understand here that it is really not all that simple as diving your annual salary by twelve months. There are certain factors that need to be taken into consideration, such as the amount of money you will be paying in income taxes every year. You need to subtract that figure from the grand total and then come to the 'real' average that will be used for your budgeting purposes.

• Have useful budgeting tools that are incorporated by default into your savings and checking accounts. It would be wise to have an online bill paying system and even automatic transfer from your savings to your checking account. Also make sure that your bank does not charge you any maintenance fees on your account and that they do not charge you excessive fees on those ATM transactions, either. If you are encountering these then you will find that it is much harder for you to stick to that budget of yours. Of course it helps if that bank you have chosen offers you a nice rate of interest as well, to boot!

• When you are making that budget, be realistic. Let's say that a lot of your expenses are directed towards entertainment. You want to be a little realistic here and not cut down the expenses toward entertainment by a whopping fifty percent, when it comes to envisioning just how much money you wish to spend on that entertainment budget of yours in the time to come. Think of it as akin to dieting. If you have been eating junk food day in and day out and decide to go on a diet in order to turn your shape and life around, you cannot begin with a liquid diet for the very first week! You will in all probability gradually 'ease' into that diet of yours, allowing yourself a provision where you can cheat occasionally in order to stem those 'junk food cravings' that have really become an integral part of your life by now. Perhaps a few months down the line, when you have been accustomed to eating healthy food and working out on a regular basis, you might then go in for that liquid diet that you have just read about in the morning newspaper today. The same goes with making a budget; make sure that you cut costs to the tune of not more than 5 to ten percent initially, and then, when you are accustomed to the change in lifestyle, you could think of going even 'more' frugal!

•   Get support from the right people. When you are in the midst of making that budget, you will realize that your entire lifestyle might be in the process of being turned around and that you need real, tangible support from family and friends who really care about you and are most supportive of the choices that you will be making. You need that invaluable sense of support, as it will only serve to fortify that decision you have made about living a frugal lifestyle and even help you to charter your course towards making it, as well!

•   Budget separately for smaller and bigger items. While you mish wish to budget on a monthly basis where it comes to things like electricity, mortgage and water, you really wish to budget weekly where it comes to smaller things like gasoline, groceries and eating out. This will ensure that any small errors that might accrue out of the same every week can be caught in an attempt to make sure that they are not repeated again. Besides, when you go over budget one week, you can spend lesser the next week in order to 'balance out' the excess expenses incurred.

• Never ever budget for 'extra money'. The last thing you want to do is to plan for that tax refund/rebate or even birthday money, in that budget of yours. If you do so you might find out that you end up spending more considering the 'cushion' you have to fall back on in the form of these things that you have made room for so easily in that budget of yours. This usually results in overspending, and you don't want to be sorry if you didn't end up getting that birthday money of yours after all, this year.

• Set those goals down in writing. This is perhaps one of the most significant reasons that you need to create that budget in the very first place. Perhaps you are saving for that dream house you have always wanted; the one that seemed so elusive all this time simply because it was way too expensive. Make sure that you write down all the goals that you have in mind when it comes to preparing that budget of yours, on a piece of paper. This will give you a much clearer definition of exactly how that budget of yours is going to be shaped, besides providing the much needed inspiration to strive with the utmost diligence to ensure that you meet all those requirements in the budget with the greatest efficiency. You want to make sure that these goals are down in writing because that will serve as a sort of 'affirmation' and form the very backbone of that budget that you will be creating.

Chapter 17: What Is Frugal Art And How Can Your Home Benefit?

Frugal art is nothing but manufacturing atheistically beautiful crafts and artistic objects, meant for general display and adoration. It involves having a passion for the finer arts of craft making that engages a very basic and minimum application of time and efforts, pecuniary or otherwise.

Frugal artful living isn't about cutting down your costs and reducing your interior décor so as to not let your month's salary vanish in a day or two. Frugal artful living is about creating and tweaking your efforts to fit an arrangement that requires minimal dedication of money and time.

It doesn't let you make compromises on the beautification aspect of your plans to deck up your home. Despite the fact that it's about cheaper plans to make your home more beautiful, it doesn't expect you to cut down on the quality of your interior décor. The result achieved by following a frugal artful life, wouldn't be different from the result you'd have gotten without following one; in fact, in many cleverly thought of frugal plans, it beats any otherwise achieved results.

Advantages of frugal living

Frugal art brings a different sort of aura to your walls. Ordinary decorations would make any home look adorable, but frugal art that has been manually manipulated turns different and samples of such cannot be found in the commercial market.

It saves your pocket a big gaping hole. The money you would have spent on pieces of expensive Chinese vases and exquisite tapestries would now be used for providing you with more useful items like a washing machine or a newly technology-laced refrigerator.

This kind of art style compliments your living room. You must be familiar with people who mismatch stuff and dump them together in their living rooms. This is a décor disaster that should rather be avoided. Frugal at, if properly created and fitted with furniture can produce a seemingly exotic living room.

You can always rotate frugal art because it's easy to make and easier to keep adding to the cycle. Because of the ease involved, it wouldn't take you more than a day or two to create and fit such artworks into your regular arrangement of rooms.

The best part about using frugal art is that it lets you take control of what goes up on your walls. Finished products bought from the market don't give you the option to have one single item that has got all the necessary traits you are looking for. Frugal art prevents you from settling for a marketing compromise.

Chapter 18: Do It Yourself Financial Assessment

Every successful company conducts regular financial assessments to see how much money it is earning and how much it is spending. You can use many of the same strategies these companies use to take a closer look at your money and get an idea of how efficiently you are spending your money.

Many people avoid taking a close look at their finances because they are afraid of finding out exactly how much money they are wasting. Finally taking a hard look at your money is going to be one of the most difficult steps you take but it's the first step on the road to financial freedom.

In this chapter, you will learn how to conduct a financial assessment on your own finances. At the end of the chapter, you will find a worksheet which incorporates all the information you will read about in this chapter. You can print the worksheet out or copy it to help you do a thorough assessment and make sure you don't leave anything out.

Assets and Liabilities

In professional terms, everything that you earn and everything that you own which has value (such as your car, your house, etc) fall into the category of "assets." Think of your assets as all the positives—anything which adds financial value.

On the other side, you have liabilities. Your liabilities include everything from your bills and mortgage payment to the money you spend on groceries and going out on the weekends. If your assets are all your positives (those things which add value) then your liabilities are all the negatives—anything which takes away value.

In an ideal situation, your assets will outweigh your liabilities. That is, you will be earning more than you spend. Unfortunately, this is rarely the case. But that is exactly where this book comes in. All the strategies you will learn about are designed to either increase your assets or decrease your liabilities.

After you have conducted a thorough financial assessment, you will have a clear picture of exactly what your assets and liabilities are so that you can start to get an idea of where you might be able to cut down on how much you spend or boost how much you earn.

Net Worth

In business terms, the difference between assets and liabilities is a company's net worth. In your case, your net worth will be the difference between how much you spend and how much you earn.

Knowing your net worth is not about valuing yourself as a person based on how much money you have. Rather, it is about understanding just how balanced (or imbalanced) your finances are. If you have a negative net worth, that simply means you are spending more than you are earning. If it is positive, on the other hand, it means that you are spending less than you are earning.

Using the idea of "net worth" can help you set realistic goals for yourself. Simply telling yourself "I have to spend less money this month" is not specific enough which makes it difficult to know if you actually succeeded in doing that by the end of the month.

Instead, you can set goals like "I will increase my net worth by $100 this month." With a clear and well defined goal like this, you have much better chance at success. When combined with a budget, you can easily look through your assets and liabilities and see precisely where you might be able to make that $100 increase happen.

Financial Categories

In the worksheet below, you will find a variety of different categories for both assets and liabilities. The categories are pretty straightforward and don't need much explanation (they include categories like housing, food, medical expenses, and so on) but keep these in mind as you create your own budget later on.

The category break down will help you to prioritize your expenses. For example, if your current financial situation doesn't include enough money to make your monthly credit card payment, you can cut from the entertainment category to fill in that gap. Think of these categories as a sort of financial map showing you where the money comes in from and precisely where it is going out.

Get out the Microscope

In order for your financial assessment to be as accurate as possible, you need to be thorough. You want to include every single little detail so that you can find out exactly what your current net worth is.

This means that before you start filling out the worksheet at the end of this chapter, you will have to pull up bank statements, paystubs, bills, receipts, contracts and anything else you have related to your finances. You will also want to find out specific interest rates (including the interest you earn on your bank accounts and the interest you owe on credit cards and other debt).

Luckily in today's society, we don't pay in cash nearly as often so your bank statement will likely have a more or less complete record of how much you spend and how much you earn. For everything else that doesn't show up on your bank statement (such as specific interest rates or things that you did pay for in cash), you'll have to dig around for the information or try to remember it as best you can.

The important thing is to be as thorough as possible. For that reason, this worksheet includes a wide variety of items (both assets and liabilities). They may not all apply to your situation. For example, there is a section for your investments but you may not have any investments at the moment. If you encounter something in the worksheet that doesn't apply to you, simply write in a 0.

The Financial Assessment

You are now ready to do your financial assessment. Get out a calculator and all the financial records you have and start filling out the worksheet below:

Monthly Assets

Gross Income   Net Income Partner's Gross Partner's Net

Main Income (e.g. -Work Income)

Secondary Income (e.g. – Second Job)

Child Support/Alimony

Social Security Income

Retirement/Pension

Unemployment Insurance

Food Stamps

Support from Family or Friends

Rental Income

Other Income

Other Income

Totals:

Total Monthly Income:

Monthly Assets/Liabilities

*This category includes things that you have to make payments on but also add value like your home and cars (you may be making payments on them but they are valuable items that you could hypothetically resell).

Present Value   Amount Owed

Monthly Payment

Home Mortgage

Second Mortgage

Other Mortgage/HELOC

Vehicle Payment

Vehicle Payment

Land/Property

401(k)/403(b) Loan

Other Payments (e.g.- timeshare, additional vehicles

Total Assets/Liabilities:

Current Debts

*In this list, you should include all debts greater than $100. You can include debts owed to family or friends as well.

Name of Creditor   Account   Number   Months LateCurrent Balance Owed   Current   Monthly   Payment   Interest Rate

Monthly Expenses

Housing $ Basics $ Misc. Obligations $

Rent/Mortgage   Groceries   Federal Tax Repayment

Second Mortgage/ Equity Line   Household Items   State   Tax Repayment

Homeowner's/ Renter's Insurance
Food at work/ school
Student Loans

Property Taxes   Medical $
Union Dues

Condo Fees/ HOA Dues   Health/
Dental/ Vision Insurance   Child
Support/ Alimony

Home Maintenance   Life/
Disability Insurance   Personal
$

Lawn/ Garden/ Pool
Prescription Medications
Hairdresser/Barber

Alarm System   Other   Regular
Medical Expenses   Clothing/
Accessories

Utilities (average)   Transportation
$ Cosmetics/ Manicures

Landline   Vehicle Payment
Laundry/ Dry Cleaning

Cell Phone   Vehicle Payment
Misc. $

Cable/ Satellite   Auto   Insurance
          Childcare/   Daycare/
Babysitting

Internet   Gasoline
      Tuition

Entertainment $
      Maintenance/Repairs   Pet
Care

Movies/ Concerts/ Theater
      Public Transport   Storage
Fees

Books/ Magazines/ Newspapers
      Tolls/ Parking Fees   Banking
Fees

CDs/ DVDs   Postage

Sports/ Hobbies/ Memberships
          Holiday/Birthday/ Gifts

Dining Out   Charity/
Donations

Vacations/ Travel
      Other: _____

Other:

_____

Other:

_____

Other:

_____

Other:

_____

Other:

_____

Total Expenses:

After you have filled this out, quickly calculate your net worth by subtracting

your total expenses from your total net
assets.

Chapter 19: The Fruits Of Frugality

What the habit of being thrifty can offer you and your family

One advantage of being rich and having a lot of money is that you can easily pay for the things that you need. You do not need to worry about making your paycheck adequate to pay for all of your bills and buying basic needs. You won't have to rack your brain just to find a solution on how to pay your debts. You will not have to live uncomfortably in a small apartment because you can afford a pent house. However, not everyone is rich. Not everyone can have this kind of lifestyle. And certainly, not everyone can afford to live luxuriously. There are some who can only get by the day and there are also some who can barely even make both ends meet.

That is why we cannot afford to be extravagant and we should be frugal and thrifty when it comes to money matters.

These days, the prices of products are higher than the sun and almost all companies are trying to raise their prices simultaneously as if they are in a race. Provided that reality, being frugal and wise when it comes to spending is a very useful skill that everyone should learn in order to survive the kind of world we live in today.

But before everything else, here are some of the benefits that you can reap out of being frugal so that as early as now, you can already see why it is important to be thrifty.

1.   Being thrifty can give you big savings.

Savings should be a staple factor in anyone's budget. It is where you get money should there be unexpected emergencies that need to be paid at once. It is the sum of money that you use if ever you want to treat yourself and buy a new gadget. It will finance your trip to a foreign country should you decide to explore some places else. Savings is really important and everyone should have one.

The good news about being frugal is that you can also save while doing it. Savings can be a byproduct of being frugal and the two almost always comes together. If you are thrifty when it comes to buying things, may it be food or clothes or anything, you can bag great savings. If you buy the cheapest yet durable variant of things, you can also save a lot.

2.   Frugality paves the way to a bright future.

Being frugal can not only give you big savings on products and on bills but it can also lead you to a prosperous and beautiful life in the future. If you are thrifty and conscious about the price of the products that you pay for, it is a manifestation of being wise when it comes to spending your money. Being frugal sometimes coincides and should come together with being meticulous. We should be knowledgeable about the different variants of the products that we use and choose the product wherein you can get the good quality that you want from the product at a reasonable price. In this way, you will be more used to and disciplined if ever there are times when it is necessary to be a little tight on the budget. In the end, your frugality will be rewarded by a prosperous future and a life without big debts. That is a good enough exchange of being tight on money, right?

3.   You will have enough if you are frugal.

There are times when it seems like your money is not enough. There are times when you feel like the cash in your pocket will no longer reach till the end of the week. There are certainly times when you would resort to skipping some meals because you no longer have even a penny to spend for food. If ever you have experienced being in these kinds of circumstances, then you must be, in one way or another, guilty of being a'one day millionaire'.

We cannot deny the fact that we sometimes splurgeour money once we receive our paychecks. We become'one day millionaires' and buy all the things that we want. But when the times comes that we no longer have money and the bills start to kick in, we almost always become stressed over the problem of where to look for cash to pay all of the bills. Being frugal can prevent this from happening to you. If you are thrifty in spending your cash, it will certainly stretch until the day that you will receive your next paycheck. Your money will be enough for the day to day needs of your family and your own and borrowing money from someone else will not be necessary.

The things that were listed above are just a few of the benefits that you can get from being frugal. There are still a lot that can only be experienced once you practice being thrifty. The benefits will come after the other so you will really find it fulfilling once you try it.

Chapter 20- Avoid Impulse Purchases At The Grocery Store

One place many of us tend to impulse buy is the grocery store. We go in for milk and come out with $100 worth of things we felt we had to have. Then you get home and there is no place to put it in the pantry or the freezer has to be reorganized to fit things and now you have clutter and frustration.

Let's face it: food is expensive. It really pays to save every cent you can on groceries. Some families spend 25% or more of their income on basic necessities such as food, shampoo, soap, and household cleaners. This can make it hard to save money and even harder to enjoy the little luxuries in life. There are several things that can be done to trim the grocery bill if you are willing to invest a few minutes.

Make a List

Just about anything you do works out better if you start with a plan. A shopping list is your plan to saving money when grocery shopping. Start by looking in your pantry to see what needs to be replaced. Make sure to include everything you need for the coming week's meals and snacks, and don't forget to add cleaning supplies and personal toiletries. Once you have your list – stick to it!

Check Grocery Store Ads

When you find store circulars in the mail, you may think of them as junk, but get in the habit of hanging on to them. Now that you have a list ready, these ads are the key to planning your shopping trip. Grocery store ads can also be found in the Sunday newspaper, but don't bother with ads from stores that are too far away. There is no point in spending an extra $5.00 in gas to save $2.50 on groceries.

With your list in hand, go through each ad and see who is advertising the lowest price for the items you need. If you see a great sale that you want to take advantage of, add it to your list. Beside each item on your list, write down the store name and price. This will help you know how well you are staying on budget.

Coupons

If you bought a Sunday paper to get your store ads, then don't forget to save the coupons too. Go through your list and see how much more money you can save with coupons. The internet is also a great place to find coupons. Just type the phrase "printable coupons" into your search bar. You will get more websites offering coupons than you can imagine.

Buy One Get One Free

Many grocery stores offer "buy one, get one free" (BOGO) deals. Some are advertised, but others will be waiting to surprise you with savings in the store. Be cautious with these deals, though. Sometimes retailers mark the price up, and then offer one for free. You don't save any money if the BOGO deal is equal to the price of buying two on any other day.

BOGO deals are a great way to maximize your coupons. If you can, try to always get two of every coupon. This way, if you can take advantage of a two-for-the-price-of-one deal, you get to use two coupons and save even more money.

Say your local grocery store is offering a BOGO deal on cereal. It is already a good deal: two boxes of cereal for $4.29. If you use two $1.00 off coupons, then you get two boxes of cereal for only $2.29. Savings like this is how some people become addicted to couponing.

Store Loyalty Programs

If you take 5 minutes and fill in a form with your basic information, many grocery stores will give you a loyalty card. The discounts you get can add up to hundreds of dollars a year. Its well worth the time spent getting it. Don't forget to have the cashier swipe your card every time you shop. Some stores will also give you coupons and other perks when you swipe your loyalty card. Winn-Dixie stores in Florida allow shoppers to accumulate gas discounts with every purchase. Who couldn't use a brake on the cost of gas?

Pharmacies

When you are do your pre-shopping homework, don't forget stores like CVS, Walgreen, and Rite Aid pharmacies. Although these stores usually have higher everyday prices, they run some great specials. These stores also have good loyalty programs and accept coupons. It never hurts to take a peek through their circular. While in the store, look for extra savings. They often have coupon books which offer additional discounts on their sale items.

Plan Meals

Your master saving scheme should include careful meal planning. This will save you as much time as money. While buying meats, think about what you will do with the leftovers. Pot roast and chicken leftovers can be turned into beef stew, soup, or casserole. Always keep storage containers on hand. Freeze your left-overs right away, and reap the savings later. This does not only apply to meats. If you save left-over corn, potatoes, and carrots, you will have most of the ingredients for next week's soup or casserole.

Buy In Bulk

Buying in bulk doesn't have to mean industrial sized cans of green beans. It simply means when you see a good deal, stock up. Non-perishable items can be kept on the shelf for a very long time, and frozen meats are good for a year. This can really help on those weeks when the budget is tight or when you have unexpected expenses. Just remember, you are trying to reduce clutter. Anything you're buying in bulk should be stored in a set area that is very organized so you know what you have at a glance and anything with a "use by date" is not wasted.

Discount Stores

Everyone knows that heavily discounted stores don't necessarily offer the best quality. However, many discount stores do sell name brand items. Household cleaners, deodorant, shampoo, and soap have a large mark-up price in grocery stores. Check the price of your favorite brands at Dollar Tree, Family Dollar, Wal-Mart, and Dollar General. It can be well-worth the stop.

Try Generic Items

Yes, some store brands are truly awful. You may not like the extra pieces of cob in your corn. However, some generic brands are as good as or better than the name brands. You just have to try them to find out. Each week, try one item in the store brand. If you like it, then you have found a great way to save money. If you don't like it, then no real harm is done. After all, you have already saved more than enough to cover the cost.

Purchasing Strategies

Here are some strategies to help you take advantage of great sales, seasonal low prices, or less well-known sources of staple items.

1. When fruits are in season and prices are lower, buy extra and freeze for later.

You benefit from this the most in summertime, when the more delicate fruits come into season, and those seasons only last a few weeks. Rather than buy pricey bags of frozen fruit in the off season, you will have your own on hand for baking and smoothies. When you get the fresh fruit home, wash and dry them and remove hulls (strawberries) or peel (peaches, nectarines). Slice into bite size pieces and spread on a metal cookie sheet. Place in the freezer. They will freeze solid in 1-2 hours, after which you can move them to plastic bags or containers.

2. If a recipe calls for Portobello mushrooms, buy Cremini instead.

Portobello's and Cremini are the same mushroom in different sizes! Cremini mushrooms are often priced significantly lower than Portobello's, however. If your recipe calls for sliced or chopped mushrooms, go for the Cremini. Save the Portobello's for grilling or sandwiches, when the large size matters.

3. If you have an ethnic grocery nearby, comparison shop for meats and produce.

Ethnic groceries often have significantly lower prices on the same cuts of meat and types of produce you find in the supermarket. This is particularly the case for items that are seen as slightly exotic in regular supermarkets (avocados, mangos) but are staples in ethnic cuisines. In addition, you can discover new fruits, vegetables, and cuts of meat that don't appear in the regular supermarket at all.

4. Comparison shop the international foods aisle for items like salsa and canned beans.

The aisle of the store that caters to Hispanic shoppers often has less well known brands of salsa and canned vegetables and beans. The contents are the same as the national American brands two or three aisles over, but the prices can be much lower.

5. Choose bagged onions, potatoes and apples over loose ones.

Skip this tip if you use these items infrequently enough that they go bad before you can use up a bag. But if you can use them up within a few weeks, or need an unusual amount for a recipe, the bags are much cheaper, pound for pound.

Moreover, you frequently get more than the labelled weight! Because the law requires that each package contain at least the labelled weight, packers will often throw in an extra or two, preferring to go over rather than risk being under the minimum.

6. In the meat department, look for the "manager's specials" that discount meat near the sell-by date.

The meat may have started to look a little brown, but it is still perfectly fine. The "manager's specials" are a great way to pick up a cut that is usually too expensive, such as some steaks! If you are eating it that day, or can freeze it immediately, these specials can be unbeatable bargains. You can even check with the meat department employees or managers to find out what time of day they mark these down.

7. If you buy milk or juice by the gallon, watch for sales on half-gallon sizes.

When there is a really good deal on half-gallon sizes of juice and milk, it can be cheaper to buy two half-gallons instead of the gallon you habitually reach for. Sales on half-gallons can go as low as "10 for $10" at one national chain.

8. Check the food aisles in dollar stores for canned goods and spices.

Spices that can cost $4-$6 per bottle in the supermarket are only one dollar in the dollar store, and sometimes in larger bottles than the supermarket. Other dollar store bargains include canned or dried staple items like beans, vegetables, and rice.

You can often find national brands of items like convenience foods and baking mixes as well. They may have been sent to the dollar stores because they are close to "sell by" dates, but often it is simply because the brand has changed packaging or discontinued a particular flavor.

9. Stock up on baking supplies between September and December.

The best sales of the year on items like flour, sugar, and specialty baking ingredients appear in the fall as the holiday baking season approaches.

Most of these items can be stored for long periods of time, so take advantage and stock up. You can get all of the cookie and cake decorations, brown sugar, and chocolate chips you need for the whole year at these sales. Items like flour and nuts can go stale, but you can freeze flour indefinitely (tightly wrap the original packaging in plastic, or move to a container) and nuts up to 6 months.

Anyone can cut their shopping bill down a lot just by planning their shopping trips and using coupons. These techniques for saving money don't take a long time, and they do pay off. Just get in line behind someone addicted to extreme couponing and you will see an expert saver at work.

Some families save so much money that they are able to live on one income. This should be enough to encourage you to go out there and see how much you can save by going shopping.

Chapter 21: General Tips

Use Reward Cards

Reward cards are a great way to accumulate points through your purchases especially if you keep an eye on deals or extra point promotions that give you the best bang for your buck. If e-mails don't drive you crazy, by being part of the reward program, you'll get e-mails telling you about the best deals and ways to get extra points which can add up over time!

Also keep your eyes peeled for great deals to spend your points on as these promotions also occur once in a while.

Make free phone calls

If you're phoning abroad, use Skype or other free messaging services that have a phone function attached. With the Internet connection that we now have and how we can buy cheap microphones, you don't need to pay for International calls. It isn't that hard to teach someone to use

Skype or a similar app on the other end either.

Always do price comparisons

Regardless of what the item is do a price comparison. For big purchases (car, house, etc.) this is a no-brainer. But even with small daily purchases it makes sense to do price comparisons, as every dollar you save is a dollar you can put to better use. You can websites or apps like PriceGrabber.com.

Don't buy the lottery

Apparently, the chances of winning the lottery are 1 in 14 million. Now I don't know about you but those odds seem horrible, regardless of what the prize is. That's why they save you're more likely to be struck by lightning than to win the lottery. Save the money that you would have put in lottery tickets and invest it. You don't need to win the lottery to be wealthy. And in fact, they say that people that win big with the lottery actually end up unhappy, usually because they don't know what to do with all that money. And out of the blue you'll have a couple hundred long lost relatives that will show up at your doorstep.

Learn to DIY

There are many things that we can do on our own that we don't because we think it's either impossible or takes way too much time and energy. But, a lot of the time doing something on your own can be a great learning experience, be a lot of fun, and save you money. So the next time you're considering replacing something or getting someone else to repair it, why not try making it a weekend DIY project?

Go to the library

Not only will you find books at the library, you'll find the latest magazines, movies, audiobooks, and discover new things. The library is full of ways to keep you excited and can actually turn into an intellectual date spot, I've seen libraries with video games too!

Stop Smoking!

I've had to have a serious talk with many of my friends that smoke and I'm happy to say quite a few have listened. If you stop smoking not only do you save money (let's admit it, smoking is expensive!), it's also extremely good for your health as well. So before you buy another pack of cigarettes, think about how much money you're wasting and the health consequences.

Avoid taking the cab

I've never been a big fan of taking the cab anywhere, and one of the reasons why is it's always more expensive than public transit. Unless it's late and you're drunk and helpless, use the public transit and save the $10-20.

Gift Spending Limits

For big family gatherings, work out a spending limit on gifts so that it doesn't burn a whole in your wallet, or worse, increase your credit card balance. The point of gift giving isn't about spending a lot of money; it's the thought that matters.

Secret Santa during Christmas and other gift giving events

Gifts are not only hard to choose but expensive. By having a secret Santa-type event, you can buy something that is generally useful and save money. Plus it's fun too!

Cancel your gym membership

Gym memberships are extremely difficult to cancel but beyond that they can be expensive. Learn to do simple exercises on your own at home or get Billy's Boot Camp!

Take advantage of free or cheap fitness classes

Many fitness classes have free or cheap introductory rates to test their classes. Take advantage of these! You can also check out Groupon to see if there are any hugely discounted fitness classes.

Educate yourself about everything you buy and repair

This is a tip that applies to every single category. If you educate yourself about what you're buying or repairing, you won't get ripped off. Let's use cars as an example. If you don't know what the market price of a vehicle is (yes, even if it's brand spanking new), you'll be at the mercy of the car salesperson and we've all heard what they're like. The same goes for when you're getting your car repaired if something goes wrong, I've heard many nightmare stories about car repairs where friends were overcharged because they didn't do their homework or didn't get enough estimates.

Get it in Writing

Whenever you're getting a job done or agreeing on something, always get it in writing. To add to my last point about car repairs, getting an estimate in writing will not only give you negotiating power when going to other mechanics to get a quote, but in case something goes wrong or they attempt to overcharge you, you will have it in writing. Unfortunately, there are many people that try to scam or rip people off so cover yourself at all times!

Make your own Greeting cards

Buying a greeting, birthday, get well, or thank you card can be very expensive. A $5 card can easily be replaced with a hand made card, which actually shows that you spent time to create the card and thought about the person you're giving the card to be making the card. Get your creative juices flowing and make your own card!

Make every 22nd of the month Earth day!

April 22nd is Earth Day where we try to make a difference for the Earth in any way! In fact if you can make everyday Earth Day, that's even better! We all know how important it is to be conscious of taking care of the Earth with all the small things we can do. Turning off the lights, planting a tree, cleaning up litter, using earth-friendly products and much more. If we all work together the impact will be unfathomable! And a lot of this can actually save you money too!

Make your own gift-wrap

Instead of spending money on gift-wrap that is going to be ripped up, why not use old magazines and create your own unique gift-wrap? This way it's unique, inexpensive and recycling!

Get annual prescriptions for your medicine

Prescription medicine is expensive and depending on where you live, for every prescription you need to pay a fee. If you have to take the same medication for extended periods, ask your doctor to make the prescription for a longer period such 6 months to 1 year. If your doctor is understanding he or she will help you out as this can lead to saving money.

Check your company benefits!

When was the last time you looked at all of the benefits that your company provides? This will vary drastically depending on whom you work for but your company could be giving you all sorts of free or discounted stuff that you didn't know about. You could be getting free massages or could be covered for something you never knew about. If your company sells a product or service, you're also likely to receive a discount on that as well! See what you're entitled to!

Don't get Divorced!

If you haven't married yet, make sure you choose your partner carefully. If you're already married do everything in your power to live a long, happy, fulfilling marriage life. Getting divorced is not only emotionally draining but it kills your financial situation too. For men, "investing" in some flowers, dinners, and ways to keep your significant other happy and your relationship healthy will reap returns you can't even imagine. Stay happily married!

Chapter 22: Tips, Tricks & Sneaky Ways To Find More Money

You should be really psyched up right about now. You know what you need to do, maybe you've downloaded a few budgeting apps, and you've made your first budget. Good for you, but don't stop there. Remember the title of this book? It's not called Frugal Living for no reason!

When you first start living on a budget, you may only be able to scrape up tiny amounts of 'extra' money for savings. Or, you may find that you don't have enough to meet every budget item every single month. Whatever the reason, you'll want to try and free up as much money as possible to pay off your debt and start building up your savings for a sweet retirement situation.

The Miracle of Saving Money

Now, there is something you should know about saving money. First, it can become highly addictive. Once you start watching your savings account grow, you may never want to touch it, so that you can look at it and see all the numbers every time you check your statement. That's okay; it happens to most people.

Second, thanks to the miracle that is compounding interest, even small amounts of savings can be a big deal in ten, twenty or thirty years' time. You may put away a measly $500 in one year, but if you're young and don't spend that money, it could sit and grow in an account for decades, reaching thousands of dollars just by accruing interest on top of interest. Who said savings accounts were boring? Probably someone who was broke...

So, to get started saving that money, after you've worked your budget, use these tips and tricks to help wrangle your money. Some will help you save money, some will help you find money you didn't know you had, and some will help you earn more money with just a little effort.

Pay yourself first

This concept means exactly what it says. Every time you get paid, bill yourself for a certain amount, and pay that 'bill' first. Put the money in your savings account and forget about it. If you don't make your savings a priority, life will find plenty of ways for your money to get frittered away, so establish this habit from the start, even if you're just putting aside $10-15 each time. You have to start somewhere, and the important thing is that you just do it!

You can make this super easy by setting up an automatic transfer to take place every payday, from your checking account to your savings account. This is super easy to set up and is so much better than trying to hide cash in your sock drawer every time you're flush with money because you won't be tempted to spend it.

Check with your bank, because some offer a service that allows you to 'round up' every purchase, moving the difference between the actual cost and the rounded up amount into your savings account. However, don't rely on that type of savings as your only savings method. Paying yourself first is better and smarter, so do that before you do anything else. If it helps, treat it like paying a bill. Just make sure you pay yourself on time, so you don't have to start calling yourself on the phone and asking when you're going to get paid...

Eat more home-cooked foods

If your diet consists mostly of things that come out of a box or a can, your body will thank you for making this change, and your wallet will, too. Research some easy, inexpensive meals that you can cook at home, preferably using basic ingredients that you can use in more than one dish. You don't have to become Betty Crocker or Martha Stewart, but cooking just 3-5 meals a week from 'scratch' can be a lot cheaper and healthier than eating processed foods, fast foods or even restaurant meals.

If you don't have time to cook every day, consider cooking several days' worth of meals one day a week, then freezing or refrigerating them so you'll have them on hand when you need them. You can do this with your lunches for work, too. Just portion out enough for each day and freeze it, then you can pop it in the microwave for a homemade frozen dinner that's far tastier than the ones you buy at the store.

Slow cookers are a frugal person's best friend. You can buy cheaper cuts of meat and cook them all day long, so they'll be nice and tender when you're ready to eat. Plus, you can just toss your ingredients in before you leave for work, then come home to a home-cooked meal with almost no effort.

Stop shopping

Okay, so you can't stop shopping altogether, but you can change the way you shop and the frequency. Grocery spending is one budget category where it's very easy to go over your budget, especially if you are cooking for a family. Start planning your meals, then buying just what you need to prepare those meals. Any other snacks or treats need to be included in the budget or made from scratch using the food you already have.

Stop going to the store 'for one thing.' That is unless you can actually walk into the store, past ten rows of mouthwatering goodies, dazzling gadgets and tempting toys. But, if you're reading this book, you probably can't resist, so just don't do it, or you could end up blowing your budget.

Also, stop viewing shopping as a recreational activity. If you're bored, pick up a book. If you're feeling down, get some exercise. Those endorphins are way better for you than the ones you get from a 'buyer's high' anyway.

Grow your own food

Start a little garden in your backyard, or in a container if you live in an apartment or condo. Grow the vegetables and herbs that you love to eat, and you'll save money on your grocery bill. As a bonus, you'll have an active hobby that can reduce your stress and give you something new to enjoy.

If you do have a little outdoor space, consider growing extra vegetables and selling them to your friends and neighbors. You could end up with a very lucrative side gig during the growing season, and if you have a green thumb, you will never go hungry.

Learn to barter

Do you have skills you can trade in exchange for something else? Maybe you have something that you don't want anymore, and you'd be willing to trade it for something that you do? The barter system is one of the oldest forms of commerce, and although it's not common today, it does still exist.

Websites such as Craigslist and U-Exchange.com are great places to go and barter your time or your stuff for other people's services or stuff. It may not be brand new, but it's new to you, and if you trade wisely, you could end up with better stuff than you had before you were living frugally.

Use coupons and watch for sales

Use this tip with caution! Too many people fall into the habit of chasing a bargain at any cost, which leads to buying stuff they don't need just because it's priced low. Use your coupons and sales wisely. Clip coupons for only the products you'd be buying anyway, and be aware that the item that the coupon is for is almost always more expensive than a generic version, even with the coupon.

You can take advantage of bargains by doing a little comparison shopping every week. Apps like Favado will let you view all the local sales paper for your area on your smartphone so that you can compare prices. You can also clip digital coupons at many retailers' websites for further savings.

Recycle

Recycling is one way that you can save money, make money and help the planet, all at once. If you aren't recycling your scrap metal, such as aluminum cans and empty food tins, you are throwing money away. Most towns have recycling centers that pay for scrap metal, and although it's not much, it can add up if you have a lot of metal to recycle. Copper, brass, and other metals can be recycled too, so scan your home for items and make some extra cash!

Another form of recycling that can save you money is reusing items around your home in different ways. Use old things in new ways to save having to buy new items. Turn boxes and food containers into storage options, turn old clothing into dust cloths or quilts and reuse wrapping paper on gifts to save money and waste.

You can also buy recycled items for less money than buying new ones. An excellent example of this is buying clothing from consignment shops. You can often find nearly-new items for a fraction of the price you'd pay off the rack.

Sell the stuff you don't need

This is how you can find 'hidden' money that you never realized you had. If you take a really good look around your home, you can probably find more than a few items you just don't use anymore. Why let these sit around, taking up space when you could sell them and add to your growing savings?

Have a garage or yard sale to get rid of the things you no longer need or want, and see how much money you can make. You can also sell items online with sites like eBay. You'll be surprised how freeing it can be to turn loose of the 'stuff' that put you into debt in the first place. Your wallet will feel better, and so will you.

DIY

If you own a home or a car, you will have maintenance costs. It's just a given. But, you can minimize those costs by tackling some small jobs yourself. Thanks to the internet, there's literally a video on how to do almost anything in the world, and they're all on YouTube.

Whether you want to tackle some minor plumbing repairs or build yourself a new set of shelves, there's bound to be a video that walks you through the process so that you can try it for yourself.

Car maintenance is another area where DIY can save you big money. Instead of paying a mechanic $25-60 to change your oil, why not learn how to do that yourself? For the cost of an oil filter and a few quarts of oil, you can do the job at home for far less money.

If you don't have the tools you need, borrow them from a friend or relative, or consider renting them from a hardware store. Be sure that you feel fully comfortable doing your own DIY, or you could cause more damage than good. If you aren't sure what you're doing, ask a friend who may have more experience than you. (Here's another time when bartering may be useful. Barter someone for their services if you can't do it yourself!)

There is more than one way to make sure that your home repairs and auto maintenance get done, and you don't have to pay a fortune for them.

Give handmade gifts

When it comes to being frugal, it can be hard to find gifts that are inexpensive but still meaningful, unless you're willing to get your hands dirty. Handmade gifts are almost always less expensive than store-bought ones, and they come with an added touch of love since you have to make an effort to create them.

Depending on who you are giving gifts to, there are thousands (or more) gift options. You can give homemade food gifts, beauty products, bath soaps, handmade clothing...the possibilities are endless.

You say you don't have any gift-making skills at all, and that your arts and crafts project always look like something the dog dragged in? No worries. YouTube can help with that, too. Also, go to the library, borrow a few books on how to make handcrafted gifts, and let your imagination run wild. Everyone can make something, even if it's just a handmade card with a gift certificate that can be redeemed for a little of your time.

Here are a few ideas to get you started:

Food in jars--These are so easy, and inexpensive, that you should be doing these for everyone on your list. There are even eBooks devoted to these food gifts so that you can find inspiration. You put all of the pre-measured dry ingredients needed for a recipe, often a dessert, into a glass jar with a lid. You write the instructions on a piece of paper and attach it to the jar, making sure you indicate whether any other ingredients will be required. Then, you wrap the jar or slap a bow on it, and you have a thoughtful, tasty gift anyone would love to receive.

Scented candles--These can be prohibitively expensive if you buy them in stores, some costing upwards of $20 each. You can make your own with a few supplies from your local arts and crafts store, using essential oils to scent them. The wax used to make candles comes in batches big enough to make several candles so that you could make one for everyone on your gift list, and they'd probably be thrilled.

Knitted scarves--Even if you have never held a pair of knitting needles in your life, you can knit. Knitting looms can be found in most craft stores and are relatively inexpensive. They allow you to wrap yarn around tiny spools set on a frame, then use a small hook to move strands of yarn to perform the 'knitting.' It sounds more complicated than it is; it's actually very easy for a beginner to master. You can get looms of various sizes and shapes so you can make hats, scarves and more.

Of course, you could always rely on your old pal, YouTube, to teach you how to knit the old-fashioned way. Scarves are pretty much one of the simplest things you can make when knitting, and everyone can use a spare scarf.

Of course, you don't have to be crafty to create a great gift for someone. Try making one of these gifts that require absolutely no crafting skills, whatsoever.

Coupon book--Create a book full of coupons that the recipient can redeem for your time or services. You could create coupons for things like a free car wash, a cooked dinner, or a back rub. In fact, you can create coupons for just about anything, so this is perfect for all ages.

Photo book--Do you remember the good old days when people actually printed out photographs and put them in photo albums for others to enjoy? Well, it's time to bring that practice back. Just go through your photos on your phone or camera, print out the best ones and put them in a small photograph album. Give it to someone who will appreciate your artistic endeavors, and enjoy preserving some of those digital photos while making the recipient of your gift happy, too.

Cook a meal--Cook a meal for someone instead of giving them a gift. This can be a great gift to give any time of the year, for friends or family. (For some reason, Moms really like to receive this gift, but only if you wash the dishes afterward, too.)

At the end of the day, it doesn't matter what type of gift that you give. Just give from the heart, and it's all good. Besides, your recipient probably wouldn't feel great knowing that you overspent on them by buying gifts that blew your budget. If you do want to purchase gifts, be sure to work the cost of the gifts into your budget!

Get involved with the frugal community

Frugal living doesn't have to be a solitary existence. In fact, there are a lot more people enjoying the frugal lifestyle than you might think. Facebook groups, blogs, forums and more exist to help people share their love of frugal living, and there's no better way to pick up new tips and inspiration to keep your eyes on the prize of financial freedom than by talking to others going through the same situation.

It can feel lonely if you are the only one in your circle of family and friends who is trying to live frugally. You may be battling feelings of jealousy, or dealing with people who don't take your efforts to save money seriously. If you don't have someone who understands what you're going through, it could be tempting to throw in the towel and go back to living beyond your means.

Frugal living communities offer more than just support and inspiration. You can generally pick up some really useful ideas that can make your journey a lot easier. Need some frugal recipes, or think you want to try making your household cleaning products, but not sure which websites offer the best advice? Ask your frugal living friends. Chances are, they've tried the things you're not sure about, so they can guide you to the best resources.

To find frugal living communities online, just do a quick web search for 'frugal living communities.' You'll see pages and pages of sites, so you should have no problem finding a place you feel comfortable.

With time and practice, you'll learn all the frugal living tricks and tips, and before you know it, people will be coming to you for advice on saving money. Learn all you can from these communities, because some day, you could end up helping someone you know to become financially independent through frugal living.

Conclusion

Now that you have read through all seven chapters, you are ready to create the perfect budget, uniquely tailored to your current situation and your own needs.

Use this guide as a reference as you start working on your budget and also keep it handy as a source of inspiration if you start to feel overwhelmed by financial difficulties again.

The most important thing is that you commit to your budget once you make it. A plan can only work if you put it into action. As your situation changes (either because you get more money or have additional expenses); you can tweak your budget to accommodate them.

As mentioned earlier, the best budget is one that is flexible enough to deal with sudden, unplanned expenses. So make sure that you include a monthly allowance for any unplanned expenses.

Once you have created a realistic budget; all you have to do is stick to it and watch your debt disappear as your savings and investments grow. With the strategies you have just learned, you are ready to take charge.

So don't let your finances be a source of stress and frustration any longer. Make the choice to get back in the driver seat and steer yourself toward financial freedom!